A THEORY OF HARMONY

A Theory of Harmony

With a New Introduction by
PAUL WILKINSON

Ernst Levy

EDITED BY SIEGMUND LEVARIE

SUNY PRESS

Published by State University of New York Press, Albany

© 2024, 1985 by State University of New York

All rights reserved

Printed in the United States of America

No part of this book may be used or reproduced in any manner whatsoever without written permission. No part of this book may be stored in a retrieval system or transmitted in any form or by any means including electronic, electrostatic, magnetic tape, mechanical, photocopying, recording, or otherwise without the prior permission in writing of the publisher.

For information, contact State University of New York Press, Albany, NY
www.sunypress.edu

Library of Congress Cataloging-in-Publication Data

Names: Levy, Ernst, 1895–1981, author. | Levarie, Siegmund, 1914–2010, editor.
Title: A theory of harmony : with a new introduction by Paul Wilkinson / Ernst Levy ; edited by Siegmund Levarie.
Other titles: Connaissance harmonique. English
Description: Albany : State University of New York Press, [2024]. | Originally published in English translation: 1985. | Includes bibliographical references and index.
Identifiers: LCCN 2023029193 | ISBN 9781438496337 (pbk. : alk. paper) | ISBN 9781438496320 (ebook)
Classification: LCC MT50 .L59913 2024 | DDC 781.2/5—dc23/eng/20230621
LC record available at https://lccn.loc.gov/2023029193

10 9 8 7 6 5 4 3 2 1

Contents

New Introduction *Paul Wilkinson*	vii
Editor's Preface to the First Edition	xxvii
Pitch Designations	xxix
Foreword to the First Edition	xxxi
1. Tone Structure	1
2. Polarity	11
3. The Triad	19
4. Consonance-Dissonance	37
5. The Natural Seventh	43
6. Temperament	51
7. Tonal Functions of Intervals	65
8. Tonal Functions of Triads	75
9. Tonal Functions of Nontriadic and Compound Chords	81
Summary	93
Appendices	
A. Examples to Chapter 8	94
B. Comments on the Text by Hugo Kauder	97

New Introduction

Paul Wilkinson

Flow down and down in always widening rings of being.

—Rumi, from Coleman Barks, "A Community of the Spirit"

In the Hindu teachings of Advaita Vedanta/Non-Duality, everything is one. "Brahman" describes the ultimate reality, the background if you like, to all experience. The seer and the seen are different. The movie cannot exist without the screen; turn the movie off and the screen is still present. This understanding is referred to today as "I," "I am," "consciousness," or "awareness." Consciousness shines by itself and has nothing in it but itself. Like the sun, it is a self-illuminating, undivided wholeness. If we were to use words to describe Non-Duality, each word would be a step away from the truth. Teachers of this understanding may need to say only a few words before the student feels this awareness. As a Zen master once said, "If I speak, I tell a lie, if I remain silent I am a coward." It requires a loosening of what has been learned, a removal of the veil of experience toward what ultimately is seeking you: coming from the generator outward, not from endless concepts inward. Some people refer to these teachings as "the Greatest Secret."

For me, this book resonates closely with this understanding. Ernst Levy may just have shared here harmony's greatest secrets.

It was an early morning in Leeds about twenty-five years ago. I had just left my piano lesson with William Kinghorn. My head was all in a spin as it was after every meeting with him. Each lesson softened the doors of perception. He would open the gate and show me a pathway. Many different paths were illuminated, but Bill had a mantra: "Teaching isn't telling." I would ask him to show me something at the piano and he would reply, "That is telling, not teaching." Lao Tzu wrote in the opening lines of the *Tao Te Ching*:

> The way that can be spoken of
> Is not the constant way;
> The name that can be named
> Is not the constant name.
> The nameless was the beginning of heaven and earth;
> The named was the mother of the myriad creatures.
> Hence always rid yourself of desires in order to observe
>   its secrets;
> But always allow yourself to have desires in order to
>   observe its manifestations.
> These two are the same
> But diverge in name as they issue forth.
> Being the same they are called mysteries,
> Mystery upon mystery -
> The gateway of the manifold secrets.

Fast forward to the year 2013 and I was watching Jacob Collier's arrangement of "Pure Imagination" from *Willy Wonka & the Chocolate Factory*. He was singing all the vocals in multi-part harmony and playing a wonderful melodica solo. He released a number of these videos on YouTube, all of which contained fascinating harmonic content. I followed Jacob's social media platforms so I could keep up to date with his musical output. In 2016, Jacob wrote a post in which he was photographed with the jazz legend Herbie Hancock. He mentioned he was having a discussion with Herbie about negative harmony. The hashtag featured Ernst Levy's *A Theory of Harmony*.

I went over to my bookcase and sure enough I had the book. I couldn't remember why I had a copy, but I assumed my teacher Bill must have recommended it to me all those years ago. I read the book and could see the relationship to the topic, but Ernst Levy didn't use the words "negative harmony." As far as I understand it, the nomenclature is credited to American saxophonist, composer, bandleader, and music theorist Steve Coleman. A year later I watched a video in which

Jacob was asked to explain what negative harmony is. He talked about how any chord in any key has a polar opposite, a reflective negative version in a given key center, just as a tree has roots.

Levy writes on page 53: "Pitch change may first be considered as a continuum. The howling of a siren, the glissando on a string, are examples embodying that concept. Now, the human mind is so structured that it apprehends the continuum by starting from discrete quantities, and not vice versa." For me, and perhaps for Levy too, this means being aware that everything is generated from a fundamental tone, pointing toward an undivided sonic wholeness. It can be perceived as two things, but ultimately it's all one. It was (and still is) this approach that was so fundamental in my exploration of Levy's harmonic concepts.

After I finished studying with Bill, we formed a strong friendship, which lasted until he passed away. I would ring him up most weeks to talk about various topics, including music, new CDs we had purchased, and our shared love of the jazz pianist and composer Bill Evans. I had been reluctant to mention the term negative harmony to him as I assumed he would have found it rather gimmicky. However, in one of our conversations he brought up the term, as another ex-student of his had mentioned it. He asked me to explain what it was. The theory immediately resonated with him, although he did not refer to it as negative harmony. He told me how much he loved Ernst Levy's harmonic theory and that he taught this concept on occasion in his harmony and piano lessons, sometimes recommending the book. Bill's teachings were full of this kind of harmonic polarity, which was also evident in his compositions. Although he didn't assign a name to this theory, we spent many hours reharmonizing jazz standards that employed this harmonic concept, particularly reflecting chords across the Circle of Fifths (more on this a bit later). I believe that's why this topic resonated with me so much, illuminating my compositions and improvisations. I really like the challenge of reharmonizing a jazz standard in real time, even if it is not always successful! I think it's fair to say that many other people felt the same about this theory; hence why the concept among musicians went viral after Jacob talked about it. It was certainly a hot topic at the music college where I lectured. My sense is it is as relevant today as it was when the book was written.

To utilize the tools in this book to their full potential, I would suggest some work in the area of loosening the constraints of your own musical education/learned concepts, however they were prescribed to you. The quality of the world that comes to our attention is dependent upon the quality of attention we bring. One of the most utilized cognitive moves in modern times is the Hegel dialectic (named after the German philosopher Georg Wilhelm Friedrich Hegel). This metatheory involves an original idea (thesis), and then an unpicking of your idea from a different architecture of thinking (antithesis), concluding by synthesizing both perspectives at a deeper level of understanding (synthesis). Every concept contains its own opposite that may have been hidden away.

An alternative metatheory rooted in Eastern traditions is often referred to as a deconstructive move, in which the layers of experience are removed in order to build a new understanding or viewpoint. So, the Hegel dialectic adds more complexity, and this second metatheory ultimately helps detach your illusory self from your thoughts, concepts, feelings, sensations, and perceptions. Why not utilize these or other metatheories while exploring this range of techniques, both in and stemming from this book, and other theories closely linked to the topic?

Axis/Centrifugal Point

Generating new chords over an axis or centrifugal point was an early concept online that caught the interest of musicians and music theorists. It certainly fascinated me, and hearing the perspective of other musicians helped to further illuminate this concept. A side note here: the words *invert*, *reflect*, *flip*, and *mirror* are often used interchangeably, in different sources, when describing these concepts and ideas; it may be helpful to assign a name or label of your own choosing to each one separately in order to enhance your understanding and clarity.

The axis point for reflecting chords is between the root and the fifth of the key center. For Ernst Levy, the fifth and the third were very important notes. The fifth being the third and the sixth overtone from the fundamental sound, and the major third being the fifth in the harmonic series. The fifth note of the major scale—the dominant—points back to the tonic and functions as a resting place. The subdominant also shares the same qualities. For Levy, dominants and subdominants are *both* dominants.

If we are in the key of C major, our axis is exactly halfway between the tonic (C) and the fifth (G) above. The axis point is then between E and E♭. I would recommend using a piano keyboard for visualization or writing it out as I have below. Begin by playing an ascending chromatic scale with your right hand, starting from the note E, and in your left hand, a descending chromatic scale from the E♭ in contrary motion. (This sequence could be spelled differently enharmonically.)

Ascending chromatic scale

E   F   G♭   G   A♭   A

Descending chromatic scale

E♭   D   D♭   C   B   B♭

Be mindful regarding the note spellings as it can make chords a little harder to find. I have written the first six notes out chromatically, after which the chromatic scale starts duplicating. Another nice way of generating this would be to plot these notes opposite each other like the Circle of Fifths but with your axis running down the middle. In fact this could be drawn horizontally or vertically, depending on what resonates with you.

I personally find it helpful to have a drawing of the Circle of Fifths turned sideways with the sharp keys at the top and the flat keys at the bottom. A horizontal line splits the circle down the middle, and I have a drawing of the visual parts of a tree with the sky, leaves, and branches in the top semicircle. The lower semicircle contains the roots and soil to represent the flat keys. This is to remind me that what is below is above: deep roots feeding from the soil, simultaneously rising into the air we breathe: the lithosphere, hydrosphere, and atmosphere (the biosphere). This is a reminder that our localized, finite mind divides objects into a multiplicity and diversity of "things." Some "thing" is only observed when we observe it; we don't know what we see, and we see what we know. In the words of Protagoras, "Man is the measure of all things."[1] I would suggest that music for Ernst Levy sprang from two fundamental sources: the internal experience, and the knowing of something via human concepts—the collective representations explored again from an inner and outer movement.

Here is the dominant seven chord (G7) *reflected* or *rotated* over our axis/centrifugal point (remember this is between the root and the fifth, so in this case it is between E and E♭), and its "polar opposite":

Original chord   G   B   D   F - G7

New chord   C   A♭   F   D - Dm7♭5 (Fm6)

We now have a Dm7♭5, which might be better named Fm6. This is a sound many are familiar with, a minor four chord. For Ernst Levy the new chord has the same gravitational pull as the original one but from the opposite side of the Circle of Fifths. Intervals seem to have a destination to resolve to a certain pitch, which we might call "home." In the original dominant seven (G7) chord our ears most likely want the B to rise to the C tonic, and the F to resolve to the major third, E. In the Fm6 there is the same kind of gravitational pull. The A♭ (from our aural perspective) wants to fall to the G, and the F (as with the original chord) wants to arrive at the major third. The A♭ is the flattened sixth (or augmented fifth) in the scale of C major. This kind of terminology, however, can be misleading regarding its functionality. Does a flat six sound like a note that wants to resolve? If so, where to? Try it and I think you will agree that, in this setting, the A♭ (G#) is functioning in a similar way to a suspended four-three resolution and therefore "wants" to resolve to the G.

---

[1] J. O. Urmson and Jonathan Rée, *The Concise Encyclopedia of Western Philosophy & Philosophers* (London: Unwin Hyman, 1991), 267.

Béla Bartók utilized the power of sensitive intervals with the Bartókean Pseudo-Cadence. He interchanged the functionality of the fourth and seventh notes without changing the interval. So, let's swap around the fourth (F) and seventh (B) in C major. The F (enharmonically E# leading tone) is the seventh of F# major. The B, which was the seventh of C major, is now functioning as a suspended fourth. It can then cadence to an F# major chord as the perceived functionality of those two original notes has changed. Jazz musicians often change the dominant seven chord using a technique called tritone substitution, also known as diminished fifth or even minor fifth. They invert the functionality of the third and seventh. In G7, the seventh is F and the third is B. If we tritone (three tones) substitute this chord, we then have a D♭7 chord in which the F is now the third and the B (C♭) has become the seventh. This can be used as a substitution or as a portal to change key.

Generating New Harmony

Let's explore seven chords in a major key before and after employing the axis point technique:

Chords in a major key		New chords
I	maj7	♭VI maj 7
ii	min7	v min 7
iii	min7	iv min 7
IV	maj7	♭III maj 7
V	7	ii min 7♭5
vi	min7	i min 7
vii	min7♭5	♭VII 7

Here they are in chord symbols for the key of C major before and after:

Chords in C major	New chords
C maj7	A♭maj7
D min7	G min7
E min7	F min7
F maj7	E♭maj7
G 7	D min7♭5
A min7	C min7
B min7♭5	B♭7

Now let's take a look at the following chord progression, using the same axis point between E and E♭, keeping the tonic chord the same:

Original progression

A7   D7   G7   C maj7

New chords

E♭ min6   B♭ min6   F min6   C maj7

It is interesting to observe that in the new chord progression we now have a plagal approach to the tonic chord: a very beautiful chord sequence. For Ernst Levy, both progressions have the same amount of gravitational pull to the tonic. I sometimes like to transform the minor six chords into minor seven chords and even begin this approach from D♭ minor on the Circle of Fifths. On the front cover of the book we see a chord progression beginning from the sharp side of the circle of fifths before returning via the flat side, a minor plagal progression.

Having now explored new harmony generated from the centrifugal point, there is a new pallet of colors to utilize. If you play jazz or pop music, this is invaluable for generating new progressions and chord substitutions. It's fabulous to try on a jazz standard; very useful for harmonic expansion. If you are playing a jazz standard with a harmonic rhythm of two chords per bar, you can work out the negative version and, depending on the melodic content, you may be able to keep the original harmony and have four chords per measure.

The axis/centrifugal concept can also be applied melodically, flipping melodies over the axis point and keeping the interval relationships the same. There are many negative polarity versions of well-known songs on YouTube.

Telluric Adaptation

As explored by Levy in chapter 2, "Polarity," let's now investigate flipping intervals in chords to generate new harmony.

Observing the construction of a major chord: there is a major third (C-E), then a minor third (E-G). If the sounds are *flipped* or *inverted* from/over the tonic (*descending* in pitch) in a C major chord but retain the same intervallic relationship and therefore build a new chord, we end up with F minor. See the diagram below detailing this, with the minor chord being formed on the left side and the major—original— chord on the right, as in the way of a piano keyboard:

F   A♭   <u>C</u>   E   G

The major third E becomes A♭ and the G changes to an F. If we flip a C minor triad we would have an F major chord:

F   A   <u>C</u>   E♭   G

If we apply the same theory to a ii-V-I chord progression in C major we create the following:

ii	V	I
Dm7	G7	Cmaj7
Em7	Am7♭5	D♭maj7

I would suggest this new progression would still cadence if the D♭ major 7 chord is followed with C major as the notes D♭, F, and A♭ create a satisfying cadence when they fall by a semitone to the tonic chord. Apart from C, these are the same notes that would be found in a Neapolitan sixth chord.

Flipping certain chords at the root is often referred to as "mirror writing." It is interesting to observe that major chords become minor and minor become major when flipping triads. Major seven chords keep the same chord quality, as seen in the example, as do minor seven chords. A chord built on fourths (C-F-B♭) keeps the same structure once mirrored (D-G-C). Chord inversions are wonderful to explore, as is the creation of complex polychords and chord clusters. You could even mirror your mirror chord!

Another beautiful mirror method would be to build chords from an initial intervallic structure. For example, a chord built on the intervals of a 5th from B♭: B♭-F-C-G-D. This could be taken a step further by raising the top note by a tone and then reflecting this by lowering the bottom note by a tone. (If the D moved to an E the lower note would then reflect this when changed to the note A♭.) This could be explored with mirroring the inner voices as well. It's a rather nice way to develop chords via voice leading horizontally instead of just thinking vertically.

Generating New Scales

Reflecting scales in the same manner as in the previous section can also be an excellent tool for generating new sounds.

If we look at the tonal structure of a major scale (T-T-ST-T-T-T-ST) (e.g., C major), and then build a new scale *descending* from the fifth of the key using the *original* tonal structure from the major scale, we end up with the following scale: G-F-E♭-D-C-B♭-A♭-G (see the T-T-ST-T-T-T-ST structure in this new scale). We could name this the following: a G Phrygian, C Aeolian, or C natural minor. The name that has been attributed to this scale in recent times is "negative major." An example of the use of this tool would be to retain the tonality of C major (in the left hand) but your melodic material (in the right hand) could be derived from this new scale.

Here is a list of alternative reflected scales, the difference here is that these are reflected or constructed (descending) starting from the tonic. I would recommend playing them in contrary motion from the tonic:

Original scale						
Ionian	Dorian	Phrygian	Lydian	Mixolydian	Aeolian	Locrian
New scale						
Phrygian	Dorian	Ionian	Locrian	Aeolian	Mixolydian	Lydian

Synthetic scales also may be of interest. These are derived from diatonic scales by altering a note by a semitone; this changes depending on which scale is being mirrored.

Overtone Scale

Let's now explore the overtone scale. It has an augmented fourth and a minor seventh. It goes by many names: Acoustic, Lydian dominant, Lydian flat seven, and even Pontikonisian scale. Some of these pitches are from the fundamental note (the first note of the overtone series, as covered in chapter 1, "Tone Structure"), the exception being the F, which is almost exactly halfway between F and F sharp. B♭ is flatter in comparison to equal temperament. Having said that, some musicians often liken this scale to notes we find in nature; it really depends on how they are heard. This scale and the harmony it generated appeared in the nineteenth and twentieth century from composers such as Claude Debussy, Igor Stravinsky, Béla Bartók, Alexander Scriabin, and Cyril Scott, to name but a few. Scriabin also explored building chords on fourths.

The overtone scale reflected from the tonic produces the Locrian natural two, also called a half-diminished scale. It's the sixth mode of the melodic minor ascending.

Levy explores chords constructed with fourths toward the end of the book. For a jazz musician this scale is essential to practice in all twelve keys. If we remove the note G from the scale, the remaining pitches form a chord called the Prometheus or Mystic chord (C F# B♭ E A D).

Polytonality and Superimposition

Polytonality, in which scales or chords are stacked atop one another, can be a very rewarding tool for generating a new tonal palette. A great example of this can be seen in the first piano etude "Désordre," by György Ligeti. It is written in two keys. The right hand is in C major and the left in B major. If you are a pianist who improvises, try playing in two different key centers. You could even explore more than two! Another topic related to this area is the "tetrachord" from Greek, meaning literally "four strings." This is where a scale is split into two four-note structures (CDEF-GABC) and the quality of the note is changed by a semitone. These could be referred to as "mixed modes." There are eight tetrachord permutations on the lower notes and four on the top pitches.

Stacking chords on top of one another creates more complex chord structures. Jazz musicians refer to these polychords as "upper structures." If you have a C7 chord in the bass clef and a D major triad in the treble, a chord with richer extensions is created: more toppings on the pizza. D is the ninth of C, and F# and A are the sharp eleventh and thirteenth. These chords can be employed in triads, but jazz upper structures generally have the third to seventh tritone interval present, often removing the root and the fifth. The tritone gives these chords their strength and stability. The most utilized upper structures are major chords two, six, flat six, and minor sharp four. This is also explored in a technique referred to in jazz as "superimposition." It involves playing superimposed chords and arpeggios, which are unrelated to the key center. For example, we could have a ii-V-I chord progression in C, which would be Dm-G7-Cmaj7. Over the chord progression musicians might overlay some different chords while improvising, such as Dm7, E♭7, A♭, B7, E, G7, C. In jazz we refer to this as "playing outside." This was richly explored in the classical tradition by composers such as Benjamin Britten, Franz Liszt, Igor Stravinsky, and Samuel Barber.

All of these innovative and explorative ideas open up a new realm of composing and improvising by *deconstructing* or *undoing* original ideas and concepts in order to find a new, deeper understanding and freedom to roam.

Interpretation of Sound

On a more philosophical note, and in a natural progression from this wealth of ideas, I personally was driven to question how the human *interprets* sound and how prior "conditioning" of our interpretation of sound affects our creative processes. In the words of William Wordsworth:

> From this green earth; of all the mighty world
> Of eye, and ear, - both what they half create,
> And what perceive; well pleased to recognize
> In nature and the language of the sense,
> The anchor of my purest thoughts, the nurse,
> The guide, the guardian of my heart, and soul
> Of all my moral being.[2]

---

[2]William Wordsworth, *William Wordsworth: Selected Poems* (Middlesex: Penguin, 1994), 68.

First, our ears perceive sound, which is then often conceptualized by the learned intellect. It is pure perception transforming into theoretical concepts. For me, this reexperiencing is the key to transcending objective limitations, a two-way process yet ultimately generated from the one. The rational mind creates order, but a musician's imagination processes the potential transformational quality to create sounds from a higher cosmic consciousness: the life force that animates it. Great music is not limited by ideas and concepts. The calling of an artist is to create, in this creation, like hovering between the polarities of a magnet, the intermediary. I don't *work* the piano; I *play* the piano. This creative act of play reflects back and forth between form and formless. The intellect has to posses the power to read without the translation.

The British philosopher Owen Barfield (who was a great friend of C. S. Lewis and J. R. R. Tolkien) called our learned intellect "dashboard knowledge." The dashboard is useful, but it is not really telling us what is happening, yet it forms the way we attend to, and view, the world. "Thinking" and "I think" are two very different presuppositions. One is alive with possibilities; the other is running dead concepts of others. Barfield called this the "Residue of Unresolved Positivism": the gulf between our inner experience and the objective world. William Blake wrote, "How do you know but ev'ry Bird that cuts the airy way, Is an immense world of delight, clos'd by your senses five?"[3]

So, are the sounds that we hear already *preconditioned* by learned concepts of others? Is there then a way that we can hear sounds with *unconditioned* ears?

The origin of the word *recognition* (from the Latin *recognitionem*) comes from "to acknowledge," to "know again." The word in Vedic Sanskrit for *ignorance* is *Avidyā*. In Advaita Vedanta, the Avidyā refers to our limited subject-object human thinking. This ignorance then veils the true self. This reexperiencing can bring into being something new that can be shared via the language of the intellect. If we can let go of the things we've learned, a conflict is removed and there is a possibility to see (or hear) something again for the first time.

---

[3]William Blake and David Bindman, *William Blake: The Complete Illuminated Books* (London: Thames & Hudson, 2019), 113.

Tracing Origins

There are a number of musical theorists and composers who more than likely helped shape and influence the work of Ernst Levy in one way or another. These theorists were interested in using our learned conceptual "dashboard" knowledge without detaching it from nature and the origins of sound. They were mindful of just (pure) intonation and equal temperament, moving between percepts, words, and concepts: a lived intuition. They were very aware of our learned limitations and were trying to reconnect experientially, exploring the infinite before the finite. They incorporated methodology, mathematics, and Cartesian modes of thought to illuminate harmony. The map is very useful, but it's not the land. Music theory could be seen as objectification, compared to the history of music, which is music actualized. We all know what happens to the wine glass if it is sympathetically resonated. The fundamental note can be heard, but increase the intensity and the glass will smash.

The French composer and music theorist Jean-Phillippe Rameau explored musical polarity in his *Génération harmonique*, first published in 1737. Some say that he instigated a revolution in music theory. It is still a popular work to this day. In this, he explores the fifth being the sum of two thirds (C-E, E-G in C major), building harmonically in thirds as a fundamental rule, the results of generating notes from ascending and descending fifths, creating two Circles of Fifths, and generating both an upper and lower series of partials. He was trying to find the natural causes of harmony. In France, he was even named "the Isaac Newton of music." The Belgian musicologist François-Joseph Fétis also explored this architecture of thinking. Influenced by the German idealists such as Kant, Fichte, Schelling, and Hegel, he was interested in the metaphysical affinities of sound. This is explored in his four orders of tonality: Unitonic, Transitonic, Pluritonic, and Omnitonic. Another musicologist influenced by the German idealists was Moritz Hauptmann. In 1853, he wrote a book titled *The Nature of Harmony and Meter* in which he conceived the idea that minor and major triads were opposites. Others that investigated these concepts were music theorists such as Alexandre-Étienne Choron, Johann Philipp

Kirnberger, Mathurin Auguste Balthasar Barbereau, Charles-Simon Catel, François-Auguste Gevaert, Hugo Riemann, Hans Kayser, and more recently Joseph Yasser and Harry Partch.

Riemannian theory—named after the musicologist Hugo Riemann—has a strong following among musicians today. There is a lot of online content on this theory, which is rooted in the dualistic tradition. His work, like Ernst Levy's, explored the polarity between minor and major chords. This later evolved to Neo-Riemannian theory, involving basic voice leading transformations. These are named parallel, relative, and leading-tone. In a parallel transformation a G major chord would become G minor, the relative would be E minor, and the leading-tone would transform to B minor.

Modern music theorists such as David Lewin and a number of others employed a Tonnetz (German for "tone network") using equal temperament. The Tonnetz first appeared in the work of Leonhard Euler in 1739. The modern Tonnetz is an infinitely expanding grid, showing the transformations of the three moves in a lattice diagram.

Otonality and Utonality introduced by composer and music theorist Harry Partch are explored in his 1949 book, *Genesis of a Music*.

The Man and his Music

We live in a digital age. Young musicians work on crafting their art yet simultaneously face pressure to promote themselves on social media platforms. In private, they know how much work they need to do yet on social media platforms they post how great they are. This wouldn't have been an issue for Ernst Levy; he composed music out of necessity, using his energy to work on his craft. Many of his compositions have remained unperformed or recorded. Music illuminated his whole being. At the age of six he gave his first public performance.

Levy was born in the northwest of Switzerland in Basel on November 18, 1895, and died in Morges, Switzerland, in 1981. He studied in Basel—the cultural capital—under Hans Huber and Ego Petri. Between 1917 and 1921, Levy became head of the piano master classes at the same institute. Four years after, he moved to Paris and earned a living as a pianist and teacher. He even became the founding conductor of Choeur Philharmonique.

Levy journeyed to the United States in 1941, where he taught at a number of institutions: New England Conservatory of Music in Boston from 1941 to 1945 and Bennington College in Vermont from 1946 to 1951. Levy was a good skier and enjoyed skiing to his classes while living in Vermont. He moved to the University of Chicago from 1951 to 1954, then Massachusetts Institute of Technology from 1954 to 1959, and Brooklyn College of the City University of New York from 1959 to 1966. He taught piano and composition and regarded himself primarily as a composer. A very gifted pianist with a formidable technique, he performed pieces such as the late Beethoven piano sonatas, Schumann's "Carnaval" and Symphonic Études, Liszt's piano sonata, and Brahms's Haydn Variations, among many others. Recordings are available for both the Beethoven sonatas and Liszt's B minor sonata. His Beethoven recordings are a personal favorite.

Levy was a very prolific composer, writing for every kind of occasion and instrumentation. He composed symphonies, sonatas, and chamber and choral works as well as various solo pieces. In 1966 he returned to Switzerland where he spent the remainder of his life. His last fifteen years were very active: composing, recording, and conducting some special teaching seminars.

Levy's music is a perfect accompaniment to this book. In his works, you can hear the musical outcome of his thinking such as the shifting of melodic and harmonic passages and the use of centrifugal orchestral textures. It is fascinating to hear his free-flowing use of meter in combination with the harmonic content. The music has bar lines but is unmetered and without a strict metric beat, involving free-flowing, complex polyrhythms. Ernst Levy explored the many colors and different parameters of tonality. He wanted to expand the tonal field, and he was fascinated with developing tonal relationships. The symphonies are particularly attractive works; the third movement from the 10th symphony is beautiful. These orchestral works are available to listen online: "Orchestral Suite No. 3," symphonies 7, 10, and 12; and Levy's last symphony, 15. There is also a CD recording of his cello concerto alongside his son Frank Levy's cello concerto.

Along with this text, Levy wrote a number of academic papers and other texts, including books. With his close friend Siegmund Levarie, he cowrote *Tone: A Study in Musical Acoustics*; the two also wrote *Musical Morphology: A Discourse and a Dictionary*. *Morphology* is a word utilized by Goethe. In this book Levy and Levarie don't describe musical forms but explore the phenomena that *makes* musical forms, the bearers of the properties. The book describes how the phenomenon of sound is the result of sound waves; whatever sounds are, they are either events or processes. Goethe believed that the scientific method, which came into being, was not the only way of looking at the phenomena. These metaphysics are still dominant today. He maintained that there was an inside to nature, which could not be measured or weighed: a distinction between the potential and the actual. Levy also wrote a book of aphorisms dealing with music, philosophy, and sociology entitled *Rapports entre la musique et la société*, which was published in France. He was also, apparently, a very fine cook.

Levy was a great thinker and philosopher. The quotations that illuminate each chapter shine with his knowing. Included are writings from Philolaos who was part of the Greek pre-Socratic school and a prominent figure in the Pythagorean tradition, a philosophy dominated by mathematics and mysticism. He believed that the foundation of everything was in the finite and the infinite. This is the great gift of Levy's work.

This way of transcending knowledge requires the power of the imagination, a quality that Levy was obviously very adept at utilizing. William Blake wrote, "What is now proved was only imagin'd."[4] What Levy imagined, he left to us in this beautiful book. He took the harmonic traditions of old and showed us a new way of seeing them. Tonality isn't an accidental feature of sound. When we hear a sound, is that sound located in or outside of us? Levy transcended knowledge by simply following his own experience. They weren't just beliefs but truths generated by the nature of sound and all that it illuminated for him. Notes are a manifestation from and in the Logos, the very nature of tonality, and the "idea of ideas" perhaps.

---

[4] William Blake and David Bindman, *William Blake: The Complete Illuminated Books* (London: Thames & Hudson, 2019), 413.

In this introduction, I have shared with you different ways of perceiving this book in the language of today's musicians in the hope that every reader can continue to drink from its infinite well. I have explored different architectures of thinking. These have been at times conceptual, constructing new ways of viewing the work. I have also been mindful of the mind's hunger for concepts and have tried to deconstruct the contents of experience in a way that I hope will provide a new viewpoint in which this text can be read from.

Whether your genre of music is classical, jazz, pop, hip-hop, or rap, there's something here for us all. Every time I read it more secrets are revealed.

Editor's Preface to the First Edition

Ernst Levy—composer, pianist, teacher, philosopher—set down his ideas on harmony in the winter of 1940–41 in a lengthy manuscript in French entitled *Connaissance harmonique: Essai sur la structure musicale du son*. The war interfered with publication. About ten years later, when we were colleagues on the faculty of the University of Chicago, he translated the manuscript into English, using the occasion to tighten and revise the text. After one negotiation with a publisher, pursued with little energy and less success, Ernst Levy (in a manner characteristic of him) did nothing more for the manuscript than to circulate a few mimeo graphed copies to a small group of friends. After his death in 1981, the efforts of one of these friends, who (like all who had read the manuscript) believed in its lasting significance, led to the present publication.

I was asked to prepare the manuscript for the printer because of my long-standing acquaintance with Ernst Levy's thoughts and his manner of expressing them. In the course of our friendship of more than three decades, we wrote two books together and collaborated on various other smaller projects. I had, moreover, frequently discussed various aspects of his theory with him. A welcome participant in many of these discussions was the composer Hugo Kauder, whose friendship Ernst Levy cherished and whose judgment he respected. It was Hugo Kauder who, in my presence, persuaded the author to replace the original term *modale* by *determinant*, the only change I have felt free to introduce in this edition. Hugo Kauder's copy, now in my possession, also contains a multitude of valuable comments written in the margins and shared with Ernst Levy who (as I personally witnessed) gratefully accepted them. For this reason, I have decided to place all these comments in a special appendix where, without interrupting the flow of the original, they will add an extra dimension to some of the ideas. In the main body of the book, all places thus commented upon are marked by a small asterisk.

A fresh idea necessitates a fresh vocabulary. The term *determinant* mentioned above is central to one of the innovations introduced and developed by Ernst Levy: recognition of the generative force of the interval of the major third. He believed, not in a total abandoning, but rather in a "fan-like" widening of traditional harmony. The third, as he saw it, had hitherto been treated as secondary to the octave and fifth; as an essential formative ingredient of the triad, it deserves to be understood as a primary force. Hence (as the reader will discover) many chords find new and revealing explanations by being "determined" in relation to the major third.

Another factor widening the view of traditional harmony is Ernst Levy's consistent application of the general principle of polarity to music theory. In this respect, he continues a line of thought stretching from Plato through Zarlino to Riemann; but none of his predecessors, I submit, ever pursued polar harmony so thoroughly and rigorously to its last logical consequences. To express in shorthand the variety of fresh relationships, a set of symbols had to be introduced; they are explained as they occur.

Professor Ernest G. McClain, Ernst Levy's friend and mine, deserves a maximum of credit and gratitude for having nursed the manuscript and the concomitant editorial efforts through all stages of its production.

Siegmund Levarie
City University of New York

1985

Pitch Designations

Throughout this book, specific pitches are designated by italicized small letters; general pitches, by italicized capital letters. Superscripts and subscripts indicate, respectively, the octave ranges above and below middle *c*. Roman capital letters refer to keys.

Foreword to the First Edition

Underlying the present essay are the contents of a book written in French in the winter 1940–41. The book, entitled *Connaissance Harmonique*, had been the result of years of studies and investigations in ha monic theory as a specialized application and development of Hans Kay ser's theories.[5] The book was never published.

Only small sections of this essay are outright translations. Much mat ter had to be condensed; whole stretches not sufficiently essential to warrant inclusion in a rather short essay had to be suppressed. In many cases, the methods of approach had to be changed to fit another language and the different modes of thinking it entails. Finally—ten years passing by not without bringing about changes—the author has found it necessary in a few minor instances to correct earlier views.

In this essay the author endeavors to present the essentials of a com prehensive, consistent theory of harmony developed from tone structure. The underlying philosophical hypothesis consists in a belief in the psycho-physical reality of tone, whereby the musical fact becomes a symbol of a physical-acoustical fact, and vice versa. It would indeed seem difficult to discover any other basis for a harmonic theory claiming to be universal.

One test of the validity of such a claim lies, of course, in the possibility of its universal application; it is a test against the monuments of music, hence historical. Another test would be directed toward the future, to ward artistic creation; this is the concern of the teacher of composition. Of both tests, nothing will be found here save a few illustrative examples. This essay is solely concerned with the making of tools.

---

[5] Cf. Hans Kayser, *Lehrbuch der Harmonik* (Zurich: Occident Verlag, 1950) which contains also a bibliography of Kayser's earlier works.

1.
TONE STRUCTURE

The Oneness was considered by the Pythagoreans to be the beginning of everything. They say that out of the Oneness sprang the Indefinite Twoness. The first, they say, is cause and motivation, the latter, effect or matter. Out of the Oneness and Twoness sprang the numbers.

Diogenes Laërtius

The raw material of theories are facts. The raw material of musical theory is music. Music is not, as some contemporary acousticians would like us to believe, "something that happens in the air." It is something that, first and last, happens in the soul. To an inner, spiritual something corresponds an outer, physical something: tone. Music happens when both are "attuned" to each other. Tone is a psycho-physical fact. Therefore no intensity of intelligence, no amount of imagination can be a substitute for the experience of music which, in music-theoretical investigations, takes on the form of experiment. We may say, then, that the method leading to the establishment of a theory of harmony—an element of music—is prevalently inductive. However, if the method might thus be called *scientific,* as the term is used in the natural sciences, the rating of the results differs radically from that used in science. In physics, the rating bears on quantities. Hence the findings are universally acknowledged. In music, the rating bears on qualities. Hence we run the risk of being subjective. It is well to emphasize that evaluation can by no means be eschewed. The substitution of quantities for qualities would be an absurd endeavor. The risk of subjectivity simply is inherent in music-theoretical research, as it is in all matters humanistic.

Tone being considered a psycho-physical fact, we obtain insights on the psychological, musical level by investigating its structure on the physical level. The data on both levels will then become mutually symbolic. On the physical level, the tone data, being treated as natural phenomena, may be expressed in mathematical terms like any object of science. The mathematical data as symbols of musical facts will, in turn, acquire a meaning of quality, of value. A number thus charged with a value meaning may be called a *musical number.* The process of investigation eventuates in the establishment of two consistent, parallel, and mutually symbolic systems.*

For its inherent qualities and the reciprocal checking possibilities which such a psycho-physical, coupled system affords, it should prove an excellent basis for harmonic research. Now, just because the musical symbolization of number is tantamount to a *musicalization of mathematics,* the freedom of the musical will is by no means meant to be curtailed by something like a *mathematization of music.* Tone structure provides basic facts and a basic framework—in short: *norms.* There is nothing extraordinary without the existence of the ordinary, the norm. *Harmonic theory is about harmonic norms.*

From the foregoing, it appears that a real understanding of matters to be discussed in this essay—an understanding in the fullness of meaning which includes both thinking and feeling, intellect and soul—can hardly be acquired by the reader without an attitude of active participation including the performing of experiments. The practical hints given here and there will prove helpful.

For the trip into the sound world we have to provide ourselves with a few utensils. Beside a sonometer, the principal piece of our equipment, we should have a supply of graph paper, a ruler, and ordinary as well as color pencils.

A sonometer is simply a string stretched over a soundboard. By the name of *monochord* it has been known from times immemorial. Although one string will do, it is convenient and desirable to have an instrument equipped with a set of strings. The sounding length of the string or strings should be such as to be easily divisible by as many numbers as possible. A convenient length, for instance, is 120 cm. A set of moveable bridges will divide the strings in any desired proportion. These bridges (triangular wooden blocks will do) should exceed the distance between the board and the string by only a very small amount, in order to avoid sizeable additional tension which would change the pitch of the tone. Graph paper tacked on the board makes measurements easy and permits convenient recording of results.

In sonometer experiments, absolute pitch is irrelevant, as we are interested only in tone relations. For reasons of convenience, we tune the string (or strings) to C. We are now ready for a series of experiments whose purpose is to show what happens to a tone when the length of the string is varied.

It is at once apparent that we need a guiding principle, for the "glissando" effect produced by a continuous shortening of the string does not lead us beyond the not very revealing discovery that pitch rises with the shortening and falls with the lengthening of the string. A glissando is a pitch motion, a continual *becoming*. A tone, however, is a *being*, an individual. Relation between tones is fixed, characteristic. Now it would not at all be true to assume that the discovery of a tone is a gradual process leading from becoming to being, from glissando to fixed pitch. On the contrary, everywhere we first perceive and deal with separate units, individuals, discrete quantities. Mathematically speaking, whole numbers were discovered—or invented—long before the "infinitely small" began to be apprehended. Thus it is but natural that we should choose the series of digits for our guiding principle. Again, after we have made that decision, two roads of approach seem to be available. We could divide and multiply the string according to the series of whole numbers and note the resulting tone relations, or we could start from the tone relations we know (intervals) and observe the corresponding string relations. The end result would be the same, but the first method recommends itself for its greater consistency and objectivity.

The series of digits being infinite, we have to limit it arbitrarily. The limiting number we call *index*. For our purpose the index 16 is sufficient. Proceeding, then, to divide the string successively by the numbers 2 to 16, we obtain the following series.:

$1/1c$ $1/2c^1$ $1/3g^2$ $1/4c^2$ $1/5e^2$ $1/6g^2$ $1/7b^{b\vee2}$ $1/8c^3$ $1/9d^3$ $1/10e^3$ $1/11f^{\#\vee3}$ $1/12g^3$ $1/13a^{b\vee3}$ $1/14b^{b\vee3}$ $1/15b^3$ $1/16c^4$

The tones 1/7, 1/11, 1/13 are not used in our tone system. Therefore we have no name for them and can describe them only by referring them to the nearest known tone. The signs ∧ and ∨ indicate that they are, respectively, higher or lower than the note referred to.

We write the series on graph paper, in one line from left to right, using one square (inch or centimeter) for each tone, and next proceed to multiply the string by the same series of digits. Now of course we cannot actually multiply the string, but we can imitate the results by using a little trick. That trick is made available through the special quality of one of the intervals we have found, namely, the octave. The octave of a tone, although being a different tone, is a sort of identity, so much so that indeed we call it by the same name. Hence tone relations may be transposed by octaves. Consequently we may begin our multiplication with 1/16 instead of 1/1, simply indicating the octave signatures of the notes we would obtain if we started with 1/1. The experimental series will thus run: 1/16 2/16 . . . 16/16; the intended series: 1/1 2/1 . . . 16/1. The result is the following series:

1/1c 2/1c_1 3/1f_2 4/1c_2 5/1a^b_3 6/1f_3 7/1$d^\wedge_3$ 8/1c_3 9/1$b^\natural_4$ 10/1$a^\natural_4$ 11/1$g^{b\wedge}_4$ 12/1f_4 13/1$e^\wedge_4$ 14/1$d^\wedge_4$ 15/1d^b_4 16/1c_4

We write this series on graph paper, starting from 1/1 c and proceeding downward.

It will be noticed that the term *overtones* has not been mentioned. Our first, ascending series is, of course, identical with that produced by the natural phenomenon of the overtones, but we disregard this fact to which we assign the meaning of a coincidence. The results of number operations (division and multiplication) applied to the string are independent of the existence or nonexistence of parallel natural phenomena. This statement is important as an expression of our endeavor to develop a harmonic theory not from natural phenomena but from spiritual principles.*

The two series are reciprocal. Musically, reciprocation means reproducing an interval in the opposite direction—an operation clearly distinguished from inversion, which is the reproduction of a tone in the opposite direction. In inversion the interval changes, but the tones remain. In reciprocation, the interval remains, but one of the tones changes. A subdominant is the reciprocation of a dominant, and vice versa; but the inversion of a dominant is still a dominant, though in position of a fourth instead of a fifth.

The so-called senarius, comprising the first six ratios, forms two mutually reciprocal triads, one major, the other minor, about which more will be said in the next chapter.

The senaric intervals are the octave, fifth, and third (in harmonics, *third* always means *major third!*). The corresponding numbers are 2, 3, 5. These numbers should at once be mentally associated with the corresponding intervals (caution: 3 means fifth; 5 means third!). Numbers multiplied or divided by 2 or its powers represent octave-identical tones. Hence, for instance, the series 2 4 8 16 . . . 3 6 12 24 . . . 5 10 20 40

... represent the tones C-G-E-, where $1 = C$. The so-called octave reduction (multiplication and division by 2) may be used for transposing very high or very low tones to within a convenient range. In general, one should keep the following simple rule in mind for harmonical operation: in a ratio representing a string length (frequencies are reciprocal to string lengths), the numerator indicates descending intervals; the denominator, ascending intervals. For example: what tone corresponds to 5/9?

1/9 = two fifths or one wholetone up (3×3 = fifth + fifth = D).

5/9 = a third down from $D = B$-flat.

Thus all tones produced by ratios formed by 2, 3, 5, their products and quotients, become known once we know the musical meaning of 2, 3, and 5, which are prime numbers. Prime numbers give birth to new tone values.

The two series represent a stage in development of "tone perspective," which we call *linear*. It is true that we chose to write the two series not on a straight line but at an angle of 90°. That was done in view of a further, planimetric development which shall now be described.

Each tone of the two series can be thought of as a generator of two new systems, analogous to the primary ones. If this be carried out systematically, we would obtain a table the center of which would be 1/1 c. By further interpolations, that table could then be developed in space. For our purposes here, however, the development of one quadrant of the complete planimetric table suffices—the one, precisely, enclosed in the angle formed by the two primary series. The interpolation may be carried out either by developing the undertones from the horizontal side of the angle, or the overtones from the vertical side. The latter method is somewhat easier.

The result is the so-called Pythagorean table. That table, of an undetermined but in any case very high age (surely anterior to Pythagoras himself), was rediscovered in the nineteenth century by Albert von Thimus, who was concerned with the historical aspects of its musical number symbolism (*Die harmonikale Symbolik des Altertums*, 2 vols.; Köln, 1868–76). In turn, Hans Kayser rediscovered Thimus (who, curiously and sadly enough, had been completely bypassed by musicology) and made the table the object of, and the basis for, intensive research in various fields. Kayser is, properly speaking, the founder of harmonics in our time.

A Theory of Harmony

Tabula Pythagorica
± Quadrant, Index 9

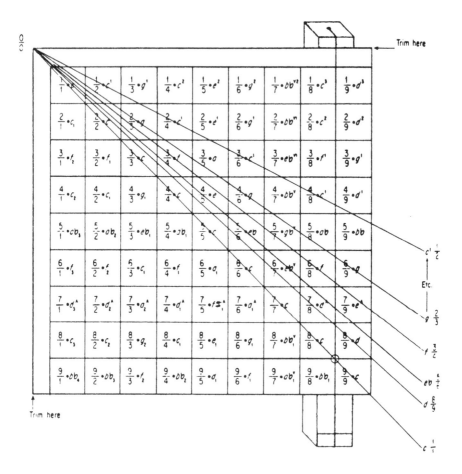

We now give a short description of the main features of the table insofar as they are of immediate interest to us.

The table is composed of interpenetrating overtone and undertone series. In view of the importance of the senarius, we shall refer to them simply as major (symbol +) and minor (symbol −) series. Every tone is located at the intersection of a major and a minor series. The series participate in varying proportions in the production of tones. They cancel each other in the diagonal 1/1 2/2.... The center of each square is the geometric locus of the tones. If identical tones (e.g., 1/1 2/2..., or 2/3

Tone Structure

4/6..., or 3/5 6/8...) are connected by a line and this line is prolonged, all such lines will meet in the center of the square beyond 1/1, logically designated by 0/0. These lines, of which there is an unlimited amount, growing with the index of the table, we call *identity rays*.

An interesting experiment may be performed showing the musical organization of the table. Make a sufficiently large table; for a sonometer of 120 cm length, a square of, say, 4 cm, or 2 inches, should be allowed for each tone. The index may be limited to 9. Trim the paper along the 0/0 line, that is, exactly one-half square behind the original series 1/1, 1/2.. . and 1/1, 2/1.... Draw a number of identity rays. Slide the table under the strings so that the upper end of the sheet is flush against the permanent metal bridge. The line to be divided is represented by the string length from the metal bridge (the horizontal 0/0 axis) to the intersection with the diagonal (the 1/1 identity ray). The string may lie over any vertical line of the table, because the rays are proportionately spaced at any point; but the nearer the monochord string to the right edge of the table, the more exact the obtained results, because of the greater absolute distance from one ray to the next. At the point where the diagonal cuts the string, place one of the moveable bridges. Each intersection of the string with an identity ray now corresponds exactly to the division of the string indicated by that ray. Thus the table may be used as a "dividing canon."

These brief indications must suffice. Those interested in getting further acquainted with the mathematical properties of the table in its various projections, or wishing to study its symbolic and philosophical implications, are referred to the writings of Kayser, especially to his *Lehrbuch der Harmonik*.

2.
POLARITY

There were from the beginning two causes of things, father and mother; and the father is light and the mother darkness; and the parts of light are warm, dry, light, swift; and of darkness are cold, moist, heavy, slow; and of these all the universe is composed, of male and female.

Hippolytus

Two theories endeavoring to explain the twofold form of the triad have been proposed: the polarity theory and the turbidity theory *(Trübungstheorie)*. Both can boast of an impressive line of champions, though the list in favor of the polarity theory may be longer. It includes the writer.*

What is a triad, and what is the relationship between its two forms, major and minor?

The polarity theorist will define the triad as the musical aspect of the senarius in its two reciprocal forms. He will further say: major and minor are perfect and equivalent consonances. They are reciprocal phenomena, and a reciprocal mathematical operation presides over their physical production. Hence they are a manifestation of polarity, one of the great principles fashioning not only the outer world of nature but also the inner world of thought and imagination.

The turbidity theorist will say that he agrees with the polarity theorist insofar as the ascending series is concerned. He will add, however, that his theory is based on the natural phenomenon of overtones; and because undertones do not exist as a natural phenomenon, he feels unable to accept the minor triad on the same footing as the major triad. Hence he regards the minor triad as a modified, "turbid" form of the major triad; and the minor third, characteristic of the minor triad, as a contracted major third.

Before proceeding to give a critical account of both theories, we have to elucidate a point not mentioned in the foregoing statements. If one admits that the triad is a consonant unit, then the question arises as to why the senarius forms such a unit, and why a break occurs after the sixth ratio (or, more correctly as we shall see later, after the eighth ratio). To this question no satisfactory scientific answer has yet been found and in all probability never will be.* It is in the nature of science that its investigations do not eventuate in value judgments. It is, on the other hand, in the nature of harmonics not only to make value judgments but to take them just as seriously as scientific statements about quantities. This means that we may boldly affirm: "The triad is a peculiar musical value. On the scientific side, it is represented by the senarius. *Therefore* the senarius acquires a peculiar value."* The risk of subjectivity in any evaluation has been stated earlier, also the necessity of taking such a risk. Yet it may not be entirely impossible to check the objective validity of a value judgment. The major part of Kayser's work is devoted to what he calls the *ektypical* side of harmonics, namely, the discovery of harmonical norms in various fields of science. From his findings thus far it would appear that there are reasons for believing in a certain objectivity of the senaric values.

We now turn to a discussion of the two opposing theories.

The turbidity theorist starts from the natural phenomenon of the overtones, which explains the major triad. Difficulty: as we have just seen, there is no "natural" reason for the limiting factor forming the senarius. A theory based on the natural phenomenon of the overtones cannot explain the break between the consonant senarius and the following, dissonant ratios. Second difficulty: the minor triad above the fundamental does not exist in the overtones. Moreover, if the viewpoint of the consonance of major as a "con-sonance" with the overtones be maintained, it can be shown that through clashes between the minor third and certain overtones we should expect the minor chord to be an outspoken dissonance rather that a disturbed consonance. Above all, the very concept of a "contracted third" is difficult to accept. Goethe has lucidly formulated the objections. He says:

> "If the third is an interval provided by nature, how can it be flatted without being destroyed? How much or how little may one flat or sharp it in order that it may no more be a major third, and yet still be a third? And when does it cease being a third altogether?"

Now as to the polarity theory, it must be admitted at once that while its principle is by far more satisfactory than that of the turbidity theory, yet the difficulties are no less formidable. The first one, arising from the non-existence of undertones as a natural phenomenon, has already been eliminated—one might say, not by untying the knot but rather by cutting it (cf. above, p. 6). The second difficulty is even more serious. It concerns our inability to hear a chord from above—specifically, our inability to hear the minor chord generated by C as C minor instead of F minor. If a hypothesis could be found explaining the contradiction between the generation of the minor triad according to the string experiment and our mode of perceiving it, and if such a hypothesis could be proved fertile and at the same time in accordance with the postulates of musicality, the inherent superiority of the polarity concept over the turbidity concept could then generally prevail in harmonic theory.*

The hypothesis I have to offer underlies the theory exposed in this paper. Here it is:

The first and most important condition into which we are born is *telluric gravity*. Gravity permeates our whole being—first of all and totally, our imagination. Now in the Pythagorean table there is no such thing as telluric gravity but only gravitation around generators—a sort of a compound planetary system with the monas as its center. About the multitude of tones we may say that they are different from one another, but we may not say that they are different in pitch, because no concept of altitude has yet entered the system. A triad pair sprung from the same generator in such a system is to be described as a pair of identical chords developed in opposite directions. We call this way of considering harmonic relations solely in respect to generators *absolute conception* (symbol ○). The system turns to a vertical position, and the tones at once assume the quality of pitch. At the same time, the two triads assume the qualities of major and minor as we know them. Looking at the major triad, we find that nothing has been changed through the influence of gravity. The generator is also the fundamental of the chord. Turning to the minor triad, we notice that generator and fundamental are divorced. Absolute conception and telluric adaptation (symbol +) are in contradiction to each other. We ought to hear the minor chord as C minor, but we actually hear it as F minor.* That inner schism between the structure and apperception is based on polarity.* We shall have ample opportunity show its workings. (Kayser has applied the concept of telluric adaptation to the geotropism of plants [*Harmonia Plantarum,* Basel, 1943]. The plant grows in opposite directions [stem-root], while the flow of the sap is unidirectional.)

In discussions about the two theories, a rather obvious fact is generally overlooked. The subdominant, not being present in the overtone series, cannot be found (when disregarding the undertones) except through an operation which is really illicit. A secondary interval (G–C) is being transposed to the tonic. With the same right one could transpose the minor third (E–G) to the tonic, which would then account for E-flat; but probably no turbidity theorist would agree, for on it would destroy his theory. Hence a curiously inconsistent situation arises where the transposition of one secondary interval—the fourth—is admitted, while the same operation is not granted to the minor third.*

Another fact quoted in discussions—this time in support of the turbidity theory—is the iridescent use of major-minor, especially by composers of the romantic period, where the minor chord of the same fundamental often appears indeed to be a "shading" of the major triad.* The suggested relationship, however, is not one-sided, so as to make minor always a derivative of major. Schubert especially offers many examples where, on the contrary, major is to be thought of as a "brightening-up" of minor. From the viewpoint of the polarity theory, we are faced in those cases with a decidedly "telluric" use of the triads. There exists, however, an inherent instability of the triad in respect to its mode, as we shall see in the next chapter.

The inner schism of the minor mode is strikingly reflected in the schism existing between its harmonic and melodic projections. In major, the congruence between the two is perfect. The melodic projection of the tones of the basic cadential functions—tonic T, dominant D, subdominant S—results in the establishment of the major scale. Now, applying the polarity principle to the cadence, we obtain a perfect minor cadence (aeolian) where all three functions are represented by minor triads. (The symbols plus and minus usually indicate, respectively, major and minor triads. Chord symbols without the minus sign are assumed to be major.) Applying the same principle to the scale, we obtain a (descending) phrygian scale, which is the perfect minor scale. This scale cannot be projected into the basic cadence; no perfect triad for the dominant being available, the phrygian scale cannot be harmonized tellurically. It can, however, be

Polarity

harmonized in absolute conception, but then it is no more telluric phrygian but telluric aeolian:*

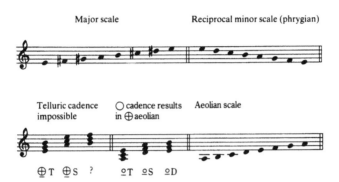

3.

THE TRIAD

*To Shang-Ti, the Highest,
To the Six Honoured Ones,
To the Mountains and Waters, and
To the host of Spirits. . . .*

Shu-King

What is a chord? An organized agglomeration of tones. What does that mean? If you depress the white keys of a piano with a ruler, you have a nonorganized agglomeration of tones; if you sit on the keyboard, you have another one. Yet we may write:

The first example shows an agglomeration containing all the diatonic tones; the second, one composed of all twelve tones. These agglomerations are organized—they are chords. What is the organizing force? A current sent through the agglomeration, creating what could be compared to a magnetic field. The tones then are perceived in relation to one or several generators acting as "magnets." The result is a whole, a specific *morphé* or *Gestalt*.

A chord is born through a certain individualization of partial tones. (We call *partial tones* all tones developed from a generator.) This may be illustrated by experiment, but of course only for the ascending series. Nature realizes here only half of the polarity principle, for the obvious reason that a string cannot multiply itself. Play a note, say, C. We know that the tone contains, theoretically at least, all overtones and the overtones of overtones, ad infinitum.* Yet that tone is *one*. Its unity is guaranteed by spatial and dynamic remoteness of the partial tones. When they are realized in their natural spatial and dynamic position, the supremacy of the generator is absolute. We do not hear a chord but a tone. The individualization is brought about by bringing the partial tones nearer to the generator spatially, dynamically, or in both ways.*

The first octave is empty, being entirely reserved to the generator, which thus rules over a microcosm. The second octave contains only one tone, the fifth. The third octave repeats the fifth, and two new tones are added, the third and the seventh. From there on the octave space is filled at an ever increasing rate.

From the foregoing it follows that the natural tendency to form chords will decrease with spatial and dynamic remoteness.

The fifth occupies a special place, being the only tone present in the second octave. In absolute conception, the generator $1/1\ c$ produces $1/3\ g'$; the generator $1/3\ g'$ produces $3/3\ c = 1/1$. In absolute conception (◯), the chances for each tone to be considered the generator are equal. We might say that the fifth is an interval with "compensated currents":

The fifth is the "presexual" interval. Hence its peculiar purity, its archaic character of something stemming from "before the creation" (cf. the beginning of Beethoven's Ninth Symphony).*

As soon as the third is added, the current is "magnetized." One of the tones of the fifth definitely becomes generator, the other one being subordinated:

The "circular current" of the fifth, however, can still be felt; hence a certain instability of the triad, pointed out earlier:

Considering now the triad, we say that it is composed of a (major) third and a fifth. *Third* and *fifth* are melodic terms, designating scale degrees. They reveal neither the harmonic relation to the generator (which for third and fifth is, respectively, as we know, 5 and 3—a source of confusion to the beginner!) nor the spiritual function within the chord.* It is therefore desirable to make characteristic harmonic terms available. They already exist for the generator and the fifth: tonic and dominant. Each term may designate either a tone or a chord built on it. The third being the interval that determines the mode of the triad, we shall call it *determinant* (Δ). The reciprocal third will be called subdeterminant (∇).

Determinant and dominant are thus the constituent intervals of the triad. The interval resulting from the relation of the determinant to the dominant is incidental, as is that resulting from the relation of the fifth to the octave. The constituent intervals may not be inverted without affecting the structure of the chord. That is to say, inverted triads are not the equivalent of the triad in fundamental position. The incidental intervals, however, may be inverted without changing the chord:

Incidental intervals are remainders. The remainder of a fifth subtracted from the octave is a fourth, and we say that the fourth is the inversion of the fifth. We could also say that the fourth is the complement of the fifth in the octave. Now the minor third is complement of the (major) third in the fifth. We shall call the sort of inversion that takes place within the fifth, *complementation;* and an interval thus obtained, a *complement* (¢). In the C major triad, the interval *E–G* is accordingly the determinant complement.

We now turn to the study of the primary cadences.

Two triads spring from a generator: a major triad and a minor triad. The unfolding of a tone in the two chords forms a stable whole:

A unilateral realization will disrupt the balance and make the chord tend toward its complement. For instance, C major will tend toward F minor, and vice versa. Hence we may say: *a major triad tends to become dominant; a minor triad, subdominant.* The oscillation thus produced is, theoretically, perpetual. The original trends can never be completely eliminated; no cadence is ever absolutely closed:

A stoppage of the "perpetual motion" may be effected by changing the mode of the intended last chord, thus introducing a sudden countercurrent:

A still more definite cadence is obtained by a combination of such a "counterblow" and an oscillation to the opposite side of the tonic:

Passing to the opposite side by a skip, the middle term being omitted, results in the classic cadence:

Probing a little further into tonality (tonality: the relationship of tones and chords to a central tone or chord called *tonic*) we add the dominants of the dominants. The functions in both absolute conception and telluric adaptation present themselves as follows:*

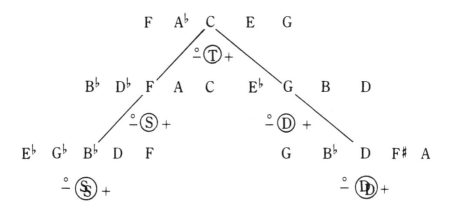

Comparing the fundamentals, note that the functions for minor in absolute conception are removed by a fifth in regard to major. This accounts for the impression that the chord of B-flat minor is somehow nearer to C major than the chord of D major. Cadences from B-flat to C are more frequent than those from D to C! This amounts to the statement that chords tend to behave as in absolute conception ○, and that telluric adaptation ⊕ is a subsequent process. By saying "the chords behave" we are, of course, referring to inner processes paralleling outer happenings. For the sake of convenience, we shall in the following always refer to ⊕, except where ○ is expressly indicated. It is to be noted that the term *subdominant* is fallacious: in absolute conception there are only dominants!*

We obtained the primary cadences by observing the latent dynamism of the triad. Dynamically considered, no chord, no cadence is every completely final. Now relations between tones or chords are to be viewed not only dynamically but also hierarchically. In that perspective, we judge the chords by their situation within a structural whole, wishing to define their rank order rather than their "volitions." Instead of dynamic trends, we shall consider fixed relations. The two concepts are complementary: dynamism without hierarchy is boundless, hierarchy without dynamism is empty.

Both the dynamic and the hierarchical aspects may be read from the table. The hierarchy is expressed in the frequency of appearance, hence the method to be applied is statistical.

A certain order based on frequency of appearance is already present in the two linear developments:

Index 6 (linear development)

Prime (T)	5 times
Fifths (D, S)	4 times
Thirds (Δ∇)	2 times

To obtain telling results, however, it is necessary first to develop the table in space. This is done by adding a third coordinate placed vertically on the center C. We obtain a series of tables identical in structure to the original one, produced by generators which are the successive tones of the overtone and undertone series of C. Such a "tone block" provides interesting but not entirely satisfactory results. By establishing three blocks, based on S, T, and D, index 8, and adding up the individual results, we get the following number of appearances of major triads (and the same number of minor triads);

C	G F	D B♭	A E♭	E A♭	B D♭	F♯G♭	C♯C♭	G♯F♭	D♯B♭♭
125	113	60	43	27	21	6	3	1	1

The middle block is designated as tonic. The order is established by fifths, it is dominantic. The fifths flanking the tonic are marked as being nearly twice as important as those immediately following (113 as against 60).

By increasing the index beyond 8, the order gradually changes. At index 9, the dominants $F\ G$ appear as often as the tonic (139). At index 10, they overtake it. The tonal unity is destroyed. That gradual "upsurge of the masses" seems an interesting and significant phenomenon worthy of further investigation. More immediately important to us is the observation that the development up to index 8, the limit of tonal unity, includes a tone foreign to the triad: the seventh. We shall come back to this point in chapter 5.

By using five blocks through inclusion of the determinants, other interesting observations may be made. For our purpose, however, the dominantic order will suffice. It represents a first organization of the tone mass, a first realization of the idea of tonality, affording numerous musical conclusions, some of which we shall now consider.

The Triad

First we have to establish the series of dominantic progression according to what we have learned. We organize the succession of fifths around C as tonic in the telluric sense, while respecting the genesis of C minor as G−°. The triads immediately flanking C± will then be G+ and F−. By listing the major triads to the right and the minor triads to the left, the dominants will appear in this order:

$$G-F-|-C+|G+F+$$

Continuing the series to the seventh term, we have:

15 14	13 12	11 10	9 8	7 6	5 4	3 2	1	2 3	4 5	6 7	8 9	10 11	12 13	14 15
C♯ C♭	F♯ G♭	B D♭	E A♭	A E♭	D B♭	G F	‖−C+‖	G F	D B♭	A E♭	E A♭	B D♭	F♯ G♭	C♯ C♭

(The figures above the tones or chords are simply numbers of order without harmonical significance.)

The primary tendencies of the major and minor triads (as exemplified in the primary cadences) create two currents in opposite directions throughout the table. Seen from C, they appear as centripetal and centrifugal. The centripetal series includes the series of major dominants and minor subdominants (even numbers on both sides). They represent the widened original cadence, creating a major zone and a minor zone in respect to C. The centrifugal series includes the series of minor dominants and major subdominants (odd numbers on both sides). We have thus:

major triads of the major zone ⎱ minor triads of the minor zone ⎰	centripetal, primary
major triads of the minor zone ⎱ minor triads of the major zone ⎰	centrifugal, secondary

The following table (see p. 28) illustrates the foregoing. It affords a systematic exploration of cadences within the dominantic tonality. C is at the intersection of four roads. Normally, one should use two of them to proceed towards C; the two others, to get away from C. That provides two normal, "falling" cadence chains, and two cadence chains in contrary

28   *A Theory of Harmony*

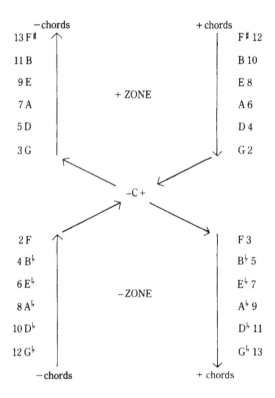

motion giving the impression not of a fall but of an expenditure of energy to keep up the motion:

+ Zone −
Normal dominantic motion

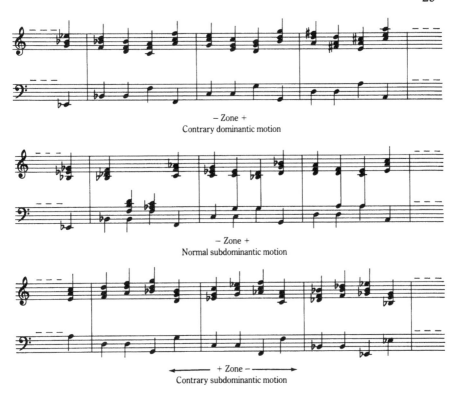

Following the numbers in their natural array, we obtain a zig-zag motion, consisting of triad pairs having a common generator:

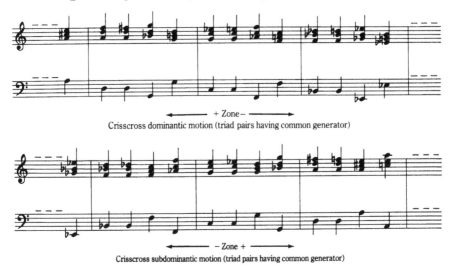

The better a cadence is balanced, the more convincing and definite it is. The balance can be read from the table. For instance:

Suppressing one term out of two in the last example, we obtain an elliptic version:

A more subtle balance is realized in this cadence:

The cadence is entirely on the minus side. It moves first toward the tonic in counterdirection (13 9 3), then away from it also in counterdirection and in symmetry to the first part. Before reaching the last symmetrical term, the cadence "lets itself fall back" into the tonic.*

These examples, one hopes, will incite the reader to make further experiments with cadences hewn from the table. At this point it is perhaps well to re-emphasize that schemes like the dominantic table are not meant to be mechanical devices for composition. What we can learn from such a system are insights into the relations between tone and psyche. The main endeavor of this paper is to show that musical norms are psycho-physical facts, not conventional fictions.

We now turn to the study of triad inversions.

The Triad

Inversion is made possible through octave identity. Hence we find the inversions in the overtone and undertone series:

$$8\ \overline{6\ 5\ 4\ 3}\ \overline{2\ 1\ 2\ 3}\ \overline{4\ 5\ 6}\ 8$$
$$\underline{c\ \ f\ a^\flat}\ c\ f\ c\ c\ c\ g\ c\ \underline{e\ g\ \ c}$$

Two facts will be noted. First, the usual order of inversion is changed, the four–six chord appearing as first inversion. Secondly, the inversions do not appear as such but, strictly speaking, as "defective series." This last observation is rather important. A defective series is one that at some point is cut off from its generator, as it were, by an index on the "wrong side." The fundamental of such a series is fictitious. If it is not, then we are not presented with a true inversion, as for instance in these examples:

In these cases, Rameau's theory is valid. Only when the fictitiousnes of the fundamental affirm itself, then the chord is a true inversion and will no more behave as in fundamental or root position.

It should be noted that in minor, things are (as usual) complicated through the contradiction between absolute conception ◯ and telluric adaptation ⊕. For tendencies (chord successions), ◯ is valid. For chord perception, ⊕ must be taken into account. Hence the following chord:

should be called *sixth chord* but treated as the four–six chord it is in ◯. The fictitious ◯ fundamental will then be f^1; the fictitious ⊕ fundamental, *a*-flat.

The general tendency of both triad inversions is that of the sixth to become a fifth as part of a new triad in fundamental position. The transformation hinges on one or two tones of the chord. There are six possible solutions for each inversion. A certain order of precedence exists, based in the first place on the greater "magnetizing power" of the exterior tones, in the second place on the normal hierarchy of the functions tonic, dominant, and determinant.

In the sixth chord, C outranks E. Hence the primary tendency: C tends to become generator, $t^+ \rightarrow t^{\underline{o}}$.

In the four–six chord, G outranks E. Hence the primary tendency: G tends to become generator, $d \rightarrow t$.

The strong tendency $d \rightarrow t$ in the four–six chord has led to the belief that the chord is what it looks like, namely, a double appoggiatura $^6_4\,^5_3$. This is not a harmonic but a melodic interpretation. While not denying the melodic aspect, we maintain that the harmonic aspect has to be interpreted harmonically. Harmonically, the chord is an inversion, and its tendency can be perfectly well explained by this quality. In primary musical phenomena, harmonic and melodic tendencies always coincide!

The same inversions on the minor side read:

In telluric conception, the four–six chord assumes the importance of its counterpart in major. This should not deceive us at the veritable reciprocals, shown in the following cadences:

See example 1 on this page   See example 2 on this page

Here is the complete cadence (reciprocal chords are marked * and **):

The beauty of this cadence stems from the absolute reciprocity of minor and major. For the sake of comparison, play the cadence in ⊕:

The balance is disrupted; the succession is trite and without beauty.

Next in order is the tendency of the other exterior tone to become generator:

Note: in four-part setting it is advisable to double the tone on whose change of function the transformation depends:

Instead of becoming generator, an exterior tone may become dominant:

Finally, the middle tone may become determinant:

34   A Theory of Harmony

The transformations are analogous for the sixth chord ($^6_4$ in minor ○).
Following is the complete table of transformations and primary successions:

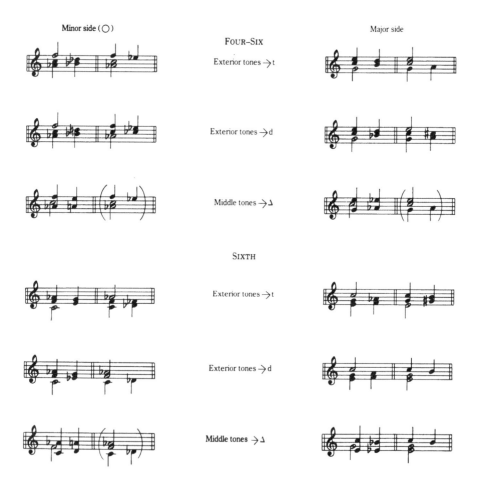

And here is a musical curiosity: a little piece consisting of all the primary successions contained in the table, in their order. Only the last two measures have been added as a final cadence; they also are taken from the table. It is surely not without significance that these successions of chords, logically developed and tabulated, crystallize in a musically satisfactory whole.

The Triad

4. CONSONANCE-DISSONANCE

The Similar and the Like would not need harmony; the Dissimilar and Unlike, however, had necessarily to be united by harmony, if it were to endure in the Cosmos.

Philolaos

Wishing to examine these terms, we begin by stating that everybody agrees as to the unique naturally consonant character of the triad. The turbidity theorist will make reservations concerning the minor triad; but this does not invalidate our statement, for to the turbidity theorist the minor triad simply is not a triad in its own right. Considering further how the expression *consonant character* could be described, we may probably agree to define it as an impression of restfulness. In musical terms, we can say that a consonant chord is apt to be used as a closing chord *(schlussfähig)*. Sometimes we observe, however, that chords which are not perfect triads and therefore do not posses that naturally consonant character are yet being used as closing chords and do give us an impression of restfulness:

On the other hand, triads may be used in a way as to produce an impression of tension, hence of imperfection, as in a half-cadence:

Summing up these observations, we say:

> The triad is consonant.
> All other chords are dissonant.
> The triad may be used as a dissonance.
> Other chords—maybe all of them—may be used as consonances.

This seems to point to two different sorts of consonance quality and dissonance quality. The first is natural, inherent in the phenomenon, and our attitude toward it is therefore rather passive. The other springs from an active attitude on our part; its source is psychological. It is manifested in currents we imagine being inducted in the phenomenon. I suggest that the concept pair consonance-dissonance be reserved for the natural qualities, and that the current pair ontic-gignetic be adopted for the parallel interpretive qualities. The following diagram will illustrate the relationship between the two concept pairs.

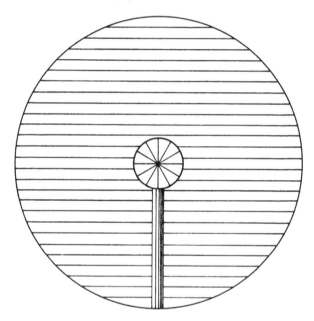

Let me offer the following explanation of the diagram. The realm of dissonance is illimited. The radius of the outer circle should be imagined as infinite, $r = \infty$. In the midst of that immense mass of dissonance lies the one consonant chord, the triad, not unlike a crystal within a mountain. Being the immediate product of the senarius, it occupies a central position. The two circles, then, symbolize the natural consonances and dissonances. Like all phenomena, chords may be approached in two ways. We might see them as fleeting appearances within an all-pervading movement. This way of looking at the phenomena we call *gignetic*. We might, on the contrary, observe the timeless quality of the instant, the *morphé* of the attitude, which is the essence of the gesture. This way of looking at the phenomena we call *ontic*. Now the two concepts penetrate into the natural realms of consonance and dissonance. To the concept of consonance corresponds the ontic view, which therefore starts from the center, covering a small part of the inner circle (of all triads occurring in a work, only the final one is "ontic," strictly speaking!) and, as it expands, a relatively smaller and smaller part of the outer circle. The gignetic quality is proper to dissonance. The ontic conception accentuates the "being" of the phenomenon, the gignetic concept stresses the "becoming." To consider the phenomenon ontically means starting from the phenomenon and "eternalizing" it. To consider the phenomenon gignetically means starting from the ever-being and "phenomenalizing" it. The ever-being is ontic. The phenomenon considered *sub specie aeternitatis* is gignetic, changing, perishable, dynamic, unreal. The phenomenon considered *sub specie momenti* is ontic. The sea considered as a whole is ontic, static; the wave then is gignetic, dynamic, perishable. But the wave considered *sub specie momenti* is an entity—real, typical, and imperishable. In the diagram, the gignetic current is represented by hatched parallel lines covering all of the two circles except the small section occupied by the ontic concept.

The range of a possible ontic-gignetic interpretation of harmonic phenomena, while being wide, still probably is not boundless. Beside theoretical considerations, recent developments in the aesthetics and techniques of composition seem to suggest that there exists a limit beyond which the norms are no more recognizable. The progressing psychologization of music had reached a culmination point in the period after the first world war, when the existence of consonance and dissonance was largely disregarded or even denied, and when solely the ontic-gignetic concept pair was relied upon for producing the desired effects of "binding and unbinding." In those days, logically enough, the triad was ostracized. Soon, however, the feeling began to prevail that one had gone too far, for it developed that artificial norms threatened to drive music into becoming a secret language evolved from a code system. Subsequently the rich discoveries that had been made in those years of frantic experimenting were incorporated into styles of writing that did not draw their principles from a mere feeling of revolt against inherent natural norms. For norms are frames of reference, without which the concept of artistic freedom becomes meaningless.

5.

THE NATURAL SEVENTH

In front of the throne seven blazing lamps were burning: they are the seven spirits of God.

Revelation 4:5

For nearly three hundred years the interval of the minor seventh has been recognized as a dissonance different from all other dissonances. Whereas dissonances in general are produced by a tone or tones disturbing a chord, and may therefore be resolved within that chord, the seventh is an integral part of a chord to be resolved as a whole into another chord. A dissonant tone is understood as a function of a chord; a dissonant chord, as a function of another chord. The seventh confers a definite function to the chord of which it is a part. Specifically, we say that:

a) the minor seventh added to a major triad characterizes it as a dominant;

b) the minor seventh added to a minor triad in absolute conception characterizes it as a subdominant:

Hence the seventh is called a *characteristic* dissonance, in contradistinction to *accidental* dissonances.

The question now before us is to decide whether or not that characteristic structural dissonance, the minor seventh, is the seventh partial.

Our tone system, proceeding from the senarius, excludes the seventh partial. The interval of the minor seventh is understood as the complement of the major second in the octave. The norm, then, is the second, the seventh being incidental. Now, the fact that the natural seventh proves too far removed from the norms of wholetones and halftones to be used in our system does not speak against the existence of another norm which would justify its use in certain cases. Our twelve tempered tones are able to represent a far greater number of tones, as we shall see in the following chapter. One of them could be the natural seventh. What we have to find out is whether or not such a norm exists.

The investigation has an objective and a subjective aspect. The first is elucidated by a study of the harmonical position occupied by the natural seventh. The subjective aspect can only be clarified through experiment.

It seems to me that two facts speak for a peculiarly "dignified" harmonical position of the natural seventh. The seventh partial appears in the same octave within which the triad is completed by the introduction of the determinant. Topological factors have already played a role earlier in our discussions, which to a great extent are based on the topology of the Pythagorean table. To the harmonicist, topological aspects are significant. The appearances of the seventh tone within the last of the three senaric octaves would indicate that in a certain measure it belongs to the triad. The statistical findings resulting in the establishment of an "octarium"—a unit comprising the first eight ratios—confirm the idea of a cohesive relationship between the seventh and the triad. We conclude by saying that harmonically speaking the minor seventh occupies a remarkable position, indicating that in a way it belongs to the senarius.

Turning to the subjective aspect, we perform the experiment on the sonometer by sounding the two natural-seventh chords, if possible including the eighth partial so as to hear the whole octarium. The impression received from the chord in Just intonation should then be compared to that gained from its realization on a tempered instrument (piano or organ). One will notice that in the tempered version the seventh stands out as a rather individualized tone, whereas in the natural compound it "melts" into the chord impression, becoming an integral part of it. The "sounding out" of the seventh chord, corroborated by the harmonical considerations exposed, have led me to the conviction that the seventh "meant" in the seventh chord is the natural seventh, not the diatonic one.

It is an open question whether in the future the natural seventh might be admitted to greater influence in our tone system. The possibility exists. But even if the seventh chord should remain the only case where the natural seventh plays a role, its introduction here is justified by the exceptional importance of the instance.

As already pointed out, the natural seventh reveals the latent dynamism of the triad:[*]

The Natural Seventh

We ask what happens when the upper seventh is added to a minor chord and, inversely, the lower seventh to a major chord:

The chord loses its unity. The seventh becomes an "accidental" dissonance which may be resolved into the chord. And curiously enough, it resolves into the natural-seventh chord:

This view is at variance with Riemann's, to whom the seventh maintains its original function whether the chord is major or minor:*

It seems to me that in this chord progression the seventh has to be interpreted differently. About that later (chapter 9).

The natural seventh, carrying into the open the latent dynamism of the triad, may touch off a chain reaction, thereby destroying the hierarchical order:

These progressions have something frightening about them, suggested by a tremendous natural driving force running loose from the ordering principles.

48   *A Theory of Harmony*

The position of the natural seventh, lying hidden in the triad, increases our understanding of the "effort" required to move in the centrifugal cadence series (cf. pp. 27–29):

In contradistinction to the triad which may assume any number of functions, the natural-seventh chord, being functionally characteristic, preserves its tendency in inverted position:

There exist, of course, numerous transformations based on the change of function of the tones composing the chord. This one is particularly well known:

This transformation, as well as others, may be read from the following diagram which shows the location of the natural-seventh chords within the Pythagorean table:

The Natural Seventh

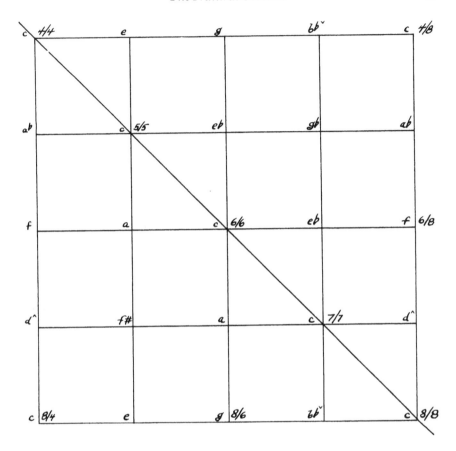

Examples:

The reader will be able to discover many other relationships in the diagram. Those that concern compound chords will be treated in chapter 9.

6.
TEMPERAMENT

Having reached this insight we are no more in a position to set experience against ideas while treating of natural science; rather we shall get used to look for the idea contained in the experience, being convinced that nature proceeds from ideas, and that likewise man, in all his undertakings is pursuing ideas.

Goethe

Pitch change may first be considered as a continuum. The howling of a siren, the glissando on a string, are examples embodying that concept. Now, the human mind is so structured that it apprehends the continuum by starting from discrete quantities, and not vice versa.* The development of mathematics offers a case in point. We see it starting from units (integers) and slowly making its way towards the continuum (calculus). If we state, "There exists an infinity of tones," we have already separated the continuum into discrete quantities. More so: we have in fact taken one tone as a starting point, and we imagine now that tone lying on an infinity of different pitches. The tone with which we started corresponds to the monas, the One, and the infinity of tones is then represented by the infinite series of integers. Thus, out of chaos, we have carved a first shape, a series. Its arithmetical aspect is one of uniformity. This aspect changes when we translate it into sound. In the series of tones we now hear, the numbers have disappeared. Relations between numbers are replaced by relations between tones, that is, intervals. Each interval has a definite character. Quantity has been replaced by quality—an entirely new element. Quantity judgments will now be replaced by quality judgments. These, it appears, create a new order within the series. The two kinds of judgments are incommensurable; yet they will be symbolically united in the number which thus acquires a twofold meaning, a quantitative one (frequency, wavelength), and a qualitative one (musical).*

Right at the beginning of the string experiment occurs what has been termed the "basic miracle of music," namely, the octave. Here are two tones, different, yet so alike that we call them by the same name, taking them to form an identity—a peculiar, unique sort of identity: two and yet one.* The quality of the octave renders possible the projection of the infinity of tones into one octave space. The octave, then, is to be considered a representation of the infinite, which may be projected into its finite space as into a sort of microcosm. Nature thus provides us, on one hand, with a tone development open toward two infinities (major-minor series) and, on the other hand, with a definite spatial framework, itself a figure of infinite space. The discovery of the octave constitutes an advance in the shaping process which began with the breaking up of the continuum into discrete quantities, into individual tones. Subsequently the infinite tone space is projected into a finite unit representing it.*

We are now provided with a microcosm filled by what practically amounts to a continuum, namely, an infinity of tones, an infinity of intervals. Having solved the problem of representing the infinity of space by a finite space, we are faced with the problem of representing the infinite number of tone values by a finite number of tone values. In search of clues, we discover the second "miracle of music," the triad. It is the third organizing factor since we started out from the continuum.

As we are approaching the concept of the scale, it is necessary at this point to open a parenthesis for a first consideration of the distinctions between the concepts of harmony and melody. Every interval name has a twofold meaning: it points both to a character and to a distance. The term *third,* for instance, designates, on one hand, a distance: it is the third (diatonic) tone from a starting point. It also designates, on the other hand, a relationship between two tones. If one of the tones is transposed by an octave, away from the other tones, the distance will become a tenth: the melodic relation has changed. Not so the harmonic relation. A third remains a third at whatever octave distance the tones might be placed. All our operations thus far have been of a harmonic nature. It seems that the melodic factor can create the tone space (through the pitch continuum) but that it cannot organize it. Organization is accomplished solely by the harmonic factor acting upon the pitch continuum. I consider melody, expressed in its prototype, the scale, to be a result of the interaction (one might say, intersection) between the harmonic and melodic factors. One has contended that scales may arise from a purely melodic operation, a division of a given tone space, say, the octave. I have serious doubts as to whether this can be done or ever has been done. In any case, it would be possible only in strictly monophonic systems, and even there the harmonic norms admittedly constitute powerful attraction points for the deviating tones. Of course, in our own system a twelvefold division of the octave takes place, and that *is* a melodic operation. But it is done by approximating harmonic norms and not as a primary, genuinely melodic operation. We shall hear more about the relationship between harmony and melody in a moment.

Turning back to our main road, we state that our present musical system recognizes only senaric values as organizing factor, limiting even these, as we shall see later. Nor were the senaric values all admitted at once. First to gain recognition was the fifth; much later only came the third. Perhaps the first scale, or at least the first fixed tones of a scale, resulted from flanking a generator by its two reciprocal fifths:

Next came the tetratonic scale. The fifth being considered a unit, adding another fifth above resulted in this:

Later, a symmetrical arrangement of four fifths around the generator gave the pentatonic scale:

Finally, by adding two more reciprocal fifths, the Pythagorean heptatonic scale was obtained:

Such may have been, roughly, the genesis of the diatonic scale.

As already suggested, the tone space is organized by the harmonic factor. In the scales just mentioned, the organizing factor is the fifth. As we already noted, intervals have definite characters, each its own. That character is, of course, a psychological fact—the response of our psyche to the interval. Whether that response is objectively founded is a philosophic question not directly related to our inquiry, no more than philosophic questions about the Periodic Table of Elements are relevant to the inquiries of chemistry. There is, however, the all-important fact that, unlike chemists, we constantly have to commit ourselves to value judgments. It may nevertheless be argued that, once the Pythagorean table is admitted as revealing the inner structure of tone in concordance with basic musical experience, and once its usefulness for theoretic-harmonic inquiries is established, we might successfully stay out of philosophic speculation, at least in a metaphysical sense. This I wish to remark for the sake of the peace of mind of those who are shying away from speculation. Stating, then, that in a harmonic sense a particular character corresponds to each interval, we may go one step further and say that obviously, if we respond in such and such a way to such and such an interval, and if that response is practically universal, geographically and historically, we must deduce a human predisposition to such a response. We may say that, for instance, the octaveness must be somehow preformed in our mind. Psychologically speaking, there must exist harmonic measures, harmonic norms. We may also say that in the series of norms there exists a hierarchical order. They begin with the octave, the most universally recognized norm, and proceed through increasing instability toward indistinctness.

Let us now remember that at first we had imagined the tone space as a continuum. Let that tone space be organized by harmony, but let the resulting intervals be considered not harmonically but melodically, as itinerary measures. Are they distinct norms or rather the melodic projection of harmony? The answer is: although they are inseparably tied up with harmonic norms, yet they are distinct from them. There is such a thing as a spatial norm. Harmonic and melodic structures are two aspects of tonal organization corresponding to two different ways of perception, of hearing. This can best be demonstrated by the example of the octave. Successive descending octaves are produced by increasing the string length in geometrical progression (2, 4, 8, . . .). The proportion, not the difference between successive terms, remains constant (1: 2). *Harmonic perception is the perception of proportions.* Take now the octave as a distance, and you will notice that the distance between successive octaves remains

Temperament

constant. Three octaves sounded together do not, spatially, appear as

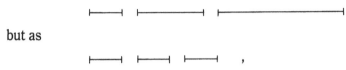

but as

that is, equidistant, just as they appear on the keyboard. Now the series 2, 4, 8, 16, . . . may be written thus: 2^1, 2^2, 2^3, 2^4, ... Our spatial hearing corresponds to the arithmetical progression of the exponents, where the proportions change, but the differences remain constant. But the exponents are the logarithms of the string lengths on base 2. Hence *melodic perception has to harmonic perception the same relation as the progression of the logarithm to that of the numerus*. Melodic hearing is logarithmic hearing. This is why, when we wish to add intervals, we have to multiply stringlengths. When adding identical intervals, we multiply by identical numbers, which amounts to raising the interval number to the nth power, n corresponding to the number of adding operations. Inversely, if we wish to divide a tone space, say the octave, into n parts, we have to find that interval which, raised to the nth power, will give the octave. This means that we have to find the nth root of the octave of 1, that is, the nth root of 2. Dividing the octave into twelve equal parts (halftones) means, then, finding the twelfth root of 2 ($\sqrt[12]{2}$).

It is clear, therefore, that the melodic norm exists in its own right, notwithstanding that it is produced by an intervention of harmony. Consequently, the spatial measures are to a certain extent independent of harmony. Spatial distortions like alterations, or the raising and lowering of leading tones, are purely melodic phenomena.

The diatonic scale is built of wholetones and halftones. The terms seem to suggest a primacy of the first over the second, and this is indeed the case. The wholetone results from the relation between the two original reciprocal fifths: $1/3G: 3/1F = 1/9D$. Notice in passing that reciprocal octaves produce another octave: $1/2 : 2/1 = 1/4$ which, octave-reduced, becomes 1/1. Octave reduction reveals the character of the reciprocation of an interval, hence something of the character of the interval itself. In the case of the octave, that character is identity. Therefore octave reduction results here in the unison. Outside the octave with its convenient tag of identity, verbal character description becomes increasingly difficult and inadequate. The fifth is certainly not an identity but rather a sort of opposition, and the character of the major second clearly shows what happens if two dominants are brought together. In any case, reciprocation and octave reduction of the fifths produce the first spatial measure after the octave or—leaving out the octave because of its very special character—the first spatial norm altogether.

We now take our primary melodic or itinerary measure for granted and presently try using it to fill our octave microcosm. Reproducing the model, beginning with 1/1C, we obtain:

C	D	E	F♯	G♯	A♯	B♯
1/1	1/9	1/81	1/729	1/6561	1/59049	1/531441

Comparing the last note, *B*-sharp, with the *C* nearest to it, we get for *C*, raising 1/2 to the 19th power, 1/524288. The difference between the two stringlengths—and between the corresponding tones—is called the *Pythagorean comma*. The tone *B*-sharp is somewhat higher than *C*. The pattern of wholetones does not fit the octave. Nor will any other pattern for which the unit is taken from the natural series of digits, because no number ever equals a power of 2, although the quotients between neighboring numbers, that is, the differences between neighboring tones, will become smaller and smaller.

We are now facing a situation which may be described as follows. Nature (the term taken in both the natural and the psychological senses) provides us with two conflicting phenomena: on the one hand, an infinity of tones and, correspondingly, an infinity of intervals; on the other hand, a definite framework, the octave, capable of containing that infinity. Among the infinite number of intervals, we select some as harmonic-melodic norms. But a row of such norms, however small we choose them (and we are not constituted so as to choose them extremely small—and if we were, the differences would appear relatively large again!), will never fit the octave. At this point a speculative remark is in order. I see in these facts a manifestation of two opposing forces, one extensive, the other formative. The first one creates extension, matter; the other, shape. If matter were allowed to multiply unchecked, the result would eventually be the annihilation of nothingness (something that in turn would be equivalent to nothingness), a sort of deification of matter, a universal cancer.

The shaping spirit opposes that evolution. The result is individuation, an entity suspended between nothingness and a-nothingness, infinity. We can detect the working of these two forces in the evolution of tone matter as well as in the genesis of the musical work, where musical matter and form are to be brought to balance each other in order to produce the individuality constituted by a work of art.

The situation we have described results in the necessity of a compromise, consisting in a deviation from the norms in order that some of them may exactly fit the octave. This operation we call *tempering,* the resultant scale, *tempered scale.* Accordingly, temperament should be viewed as an attempt to represent the indefinite within the definite. This is done by what technically looks like, and in fact is, a compromise; but it is really more and better than that. It is a stylization of matter and as such confers to the very material of music, the scale, the dignity of an art product. It thereby affirms that music is, before and above all, a matter of spirit and not of acoustics in the engineer's sense. Music—as we said at the onset—is not primarily "something that happens in the air." It is something that happens in the human soul on the basis of a response to universal norms expressed in the tone structure.

Like all norms (in contradistinction to laws), the scale allows for approximations, for interpretations. Were it not so, no music-making would be possible, for exact intonation exists only theoretically. Tones, intervals, chords we hear are mere suggestions of what is meant we should hear. As in geometry, we perceive the norms through imperfect figures. We mentally correct the impressions received through the sense of hearing. That correction is always carried out in the direction of some norm, some measure. What are the norms suggested by our equally-tempered twelve-tone scale?

Those who compose in the so-called twelve-tone system take the intervals at their face value. No interpretation is allowed. The tempered intervals themselves are considered to be the norms. Anything suggesting a comparison with Just intonation is to be avoided. In the heyday of twelve-tone music, the triad was declared taboo. This suggests that even in the minds of twelve-tone composers, some difficulty exists as to the acceptance of tempered norms. For were it simply a question of a plurality of norms, discarding earlier norms altogether would seem unreasonable. In certain works of that school, a plurality of norms appears

60   *A Theory of Harmony*

indeed to have been accepted. Still, it is an open question whether any and every device arbitrarily chosen will be accepted as a norm in due course of time. Indeed, it would mean that norms are nothing genuine and unavoidable, nothing deeply connected with the structure of our psyche or of tone. It would mean, on the contrary, that we may be conditioned to anything we choose being conditioned to. This is, of course, the viewpoint of behaviorism (a materialistic view) applied to music.*

Something entirely different is a concept of plurality of such norms as are contained in the tone structure. These indeed are not made but discovered and thenceforth never discarded. On this point I part opinion with Yasser's most brilliant theory. I experience rather serious difficulties, both musical and intellectual, imagining that at some time in the future the "octaveness" of the octave, the "fifthness" of the fifth, or the "thirdness" of the third will have disappeared, together with the "primeness" of the unison, the necessity of temperament, and—in short—the bases of music as we know it. On the other hand, there cannot be any doubt that a progressive discovery of norms is taking place. We learn it from history, and there is no reason to believe that the process will stop short of the limitation our sense of hearing imposes upon us. However, if the tone structure as expressed in the Pythagorean table is a psychological fact (as I believe it is), the hierarchical order of norms will be preserved. The "triadness," the "majorness," and so forth, will remain the specific values as which they appear to us today.

We thus do not take the tempered intervals to *be* norms, but we hold that they *suggest* norms, and we again ask the question: "What norms are being suggested?"

The list of tones indicated by our notation, including extreme cases, runs as follows:

$$b\sharp \quad c\sharp \quad c^{\times} \quad d\sharp \quad d^{\times} \quad e\sharp \quad f\sharp \quad f^{\times} \quad g\sharp \quad g^{\times} \quad a\sharp \quad a^{\times}$$
$$c \qquad d \qquad e \quad f \qquad g \qquad a \qquad b$$
$$d^{\flat\flat} \quad d^{\flat} \quad e^{\flat\flat} \quad e^{\flat} \quad f^{\flat} \quad g^{\flat\flat} \quad g^{\flat} \quad a^{\flat\flat} \quad a^{\flat} \quad b^{\flat\flat} \quad b^{\flat} \quad c^{\flat}$$

There are 31 notes. Some of them occur rarely, if ever. Omitting all double-sharps and double-flats, we are still left with 21 notes—nearly twice the amount of available tones. These notes are obtained by developing the senarius, while excluding all nonsenaric or "ekmelic" values. Is it possible to suggest them all through the tempered scale? We know that

Temperament

it is not. Now, it is generally admitted that we are able to perceive differences as small as 1/6 or 1/8 of the syntonic comma, hence the question is not one of limitation of sense perception, but entirely one of limitation of the suggestive power of the tempered scale. The following tabulation (courtesy Dr. Eli Sternberg) is offered to enable the reader to test his own perceptive faculty of micro-intervals on a monochord (c = 60 cm):

$$\sqrt[6]{81/80} = 1.002072$$
$$\sqrt[8]{81/80} = 1.001554$$

Syntonic Comma:	60 : 60.75 cm
1/6 Syntonic Comma:	60: 60.12 cm
2/6 Syntonic Comma:	60: 60.25 cm
3/6 Syntonic Comma:	60: 60.37 cm
1/8 Syntonic Comma:	60: 60.09 cm
2/8 Syntonic Comma:	60: 60.19 cm
3/8 Syntonic Comma:	60: 60.28 cm

The "margin of interpretation" of a given number of tempered tones within the octave simply cannot be widened indefinitely. Though the margin is naturally somewhat elastic, we may nevertheless determine its limits with fair accuracy, by reasoning as follows.

Our smallest measure is the halftone. Looking at the twelve tones from a structural viewpoint, we consider the following selective aspect of the Pythagorean table:

				1/45f♯
5/3e♭	3/3c	1/3g	1/9d	1/15b
5/1a♭	3/1f	1/1c	1/3g	1/5e
15/1d♭	9/1b♭	3/1f	3/3c	3/5a
45/1g♭				

The wholetone results from the relation between two reciprocal fifths.

The halftone results from the relation between a fifth and the reciprocal third: 1/3: 5/1 = 1/15. The 1/15 relations in the table are shown in the following diagram:

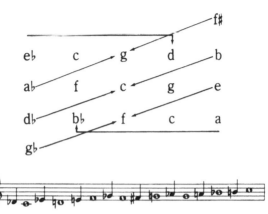

The arrangement may be thought of as the result of the interpenetration of two scales, which could be called supra-major and infra-minor:

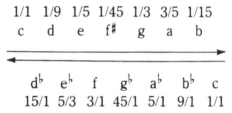

The diatonic halftone, not the chromatic one, is our smallest measure. Musically, chromatic intervals are measured by relating them to diatonic ones. Examples: for C–C♯ the *tertium comparationis* is *D*; for C–F♯, the *tertium comparationis* is *G*; for C–(down) G♯, the *tertium comparationis* is *A*. The halftone from C up, when presented out of context, will always be interpreted as a minor second, never as an augmented prime!

As to chords and keys, matters are more complicated, because one tone of a chord may have a distant relationship while that between fundamentals or generators may be close. Thus in our system oriented on C, C-sharp minor is accepted more easily than D-flat minor because of the note *F*-flat occuring in the latter chord. D-flat minor as a key is even more difficult to apprehend because of the *B*-double flat occuring in the subdominant. On the contrary, C-sharp major is less easily accepted than D-flat major, because of the *E*-sharp, and so forth. It all amounts to the statement that by and large the tones contained in the keys of F-sharp major and G-flat major constitute the limits of our tonal system as suggested by the temperament of twelve tones. This is, of course, no great discovery but rather confirms the general practice of bending the spiral of fifths into a circle at precisely this point.

On the other hand, the discovery of norms smaller than the halftone is entirely within the range of possibilities. It is not the purpose of this paper to discuss such futuristic prospects. But it may perhaps be well to state some principles that would guide us in such investigations and in fact have been a guide to myself when I was probing into the microtonic world.

First, let us remember that whatever the new scale may be, it should consist in a further penetration into tone structure rather than in a discarding of previous discoveries. Next, it is clear, after what has been said, that any new scale that may be found will eventually have to be tempered. Above all, the new building stones must not be found by dividing the octave by some figure higher than twelve but by discovering new harmonic norms. Tempered intervals never can be norms. Once the norm is found, then the octave will be divided by the appropriate figure for the purpose of fitting the norm in the octave. Thus a new tempered scale will be produced.

It seems to me that attempts of bringing into use smaller intervals than the halftone have failed so far, precisely because the problem was approached from the wrong end. The halftone is not the result of a division of the octave into twelve parts. Likewise, a new primary interval will not be found by splitting the halftone or the wholetone.

7. TONAL FUNCTIONS OF INTERVALS

Were there no tones of different pitch, there could be no harmony.

Heraclitus

In the Pythagorean table, the two outer series, giving birth to the multitude of tones, are generated by the monas (1/1) and again are held together and united by it (diagonal 2/2, 3/3, . . .). Thus the table is what we should call a tonal structure, an image of tonality.

The harmonic measures are projected into the microcosm of the octave and transformed into spatial measures which, subsequently, acquire a certain autonomy. Upon the shaping of melody or polyphony, the rules of harmony have but an indirect bearing. Harmony springs from tone, the scale from harmony, melody from the scale, and polyphony from melody. Polyphony may be viewed as the loftiest, most spiritualized part of the tonal organism.

Only the harmonic aspect of tonality concerns us here. In the present chapter we try to obtain insight into the primary harmonic relations of tones—that relation which determines the original and unique character of each interval, hence its place within the harmonic tonality. The relations thus established are then fixed in an adequate nomenclature represented by symbols. The nomenclature will often appear somewhat clumsy. Unfortunately this cannot be avoided as the complications of the relationships increase. However, an essential complication does not exclude an apparent simplicity. The perception of a tree, an animal, or a human being is "simple." They appear as morphological entities *(Gestalt)*. Also, we may perceive relations intuitively which it might be laborious to apprehend intellectually. The proposed nomenclature endeavors to capture the intimate structure of the harmonic entity. For certain practical purposes one can without inconvenience revert to the usual spatial nomenclature. For investigations into the real harmonic structure, however, adequate symbols can hardly be dispensed with.

A few examples will disclose the inadequacy of the current nomenclature. The inverted determinant is called *minor sixth,* a purely spatial term, not suggestive of a relationship with the major third. On the contrary, the terms *major second* and *minor second* suggest a relationship between the two which, harmonically speaking, in fact does not exist. Above all, the terms suggesting alteration have nothing to do with harmonic concepts, where augmented seconds or diminished fifths simply do not exist. In harmonic terms, there is no such thing as an altered chord. We touched upon that point earlier (cf. p. 57). Whenever we speak of an altered tone or an altered interval, we are referring to an non-altered state as the true harmonic relationship; hence the alteration is a spatial distortion of a harmonic entity. But if we take the altered state to be a harmonic entity, then the term becomes absurd. Alteration is a melodic term, to be banned from a harmonic vocabulary.

It has been said that our musical system is based on the senarius. This definition is somewhat too inclusive. The term *senarius* has two meanings, a narrow one and a wider one. The first is literal, referring to the first six numbers, that is, musically to the triad. The second includes all numbers derived from the first six, the application of which therefore has to be limited by an index. Now, our system is based on the triad, which to us is the measure of all things harmonic and hence melodic. In the Pythagorean system the supreme measure was the *quaternarius*. The scale thus obtained (from fifths only) is excellent from a melodic viewpoint, the only one that mattered in antiquity. Even today we apply the Pythagorean third, in fact or mentally, whenever we use the halftone melodically, that is, whenever one of the two tones is considered a leading tone. The Pythagorean scale is perfect also inasmuch as only two measures appear: a wholetone of 8/9 and a halftone of 243/256. In the Pythagorean system, the fifth plays the role of our triad. It serves as a model to be reproduced symmetrically until the tones thus obtained form a scale. We, on the other hand, take the triad as a model, reproducing it symmetrically until the tones thus obtained form a scale. The Pythagorean progression of fifths was carried out symmetrically up and down to 3^3 (not, as is sometimes explained, upward to 3^5 and downward to 3^1), thus:

E-flat—*B*-flat—*F*—*C*—*G*—*D*—*A*

In the scale produced by these notes (C dorian), one considered the two different step models the building stones of the melodic system, disregarding other occurring relationships or a least considering them secondary. It is possible that even the halftone was considered a resulting interval, a fact to which the term *limma* ("leftover") seems to point. In our system, the triad model is also reproduced symmetrically, but just once (S T D). The presence of a second generating ration (the number 5) complicates matters considerably. As far as the fifth is concerned, the index of the development of the senaric series could be fixed at 9 (*D* upward, *B*-flat downward). But the third of the dominants has the ratio fifth plus third=3 × 5=15 (*B* upward, *D*-flat downward). The overall index for the diatonic scale as produced by the three functions is therefore 16. In this scale, there exists only one kind of semitone: 15/16; but there are two different wholetones: 8/9 (*C–D*, *F–G*, *A–B*) and 9/10 (*D–E*, *G–A*). Through the introduction of the third, the semitone, now not a leftover but a norm in its own right, can no longer act as an absorber of the difference between the series and the octave. As to the two wholetones, we disregard the smaller in favor of the primary one resulting from the dominant-relationship. To us, 8/9 is the wholetone, and 9/10 the approximation. Reproduction of the triad model (major and minor) on the tones of the scale produces a multitude of further ratios, exceeding the original index of 16. As we have seen, the limit of that process is set (but only approximately so) by the impossibility of representing deviating values through tempered intervals.

From all this we may learn:

1) The representation of an open system through a closed one (temperament) is a precarious affair. The closing of the system through the identification of *F*-sharp and *G*-flat in the circle of fifths is one of those defenses man erects against the anguish of infinity and chaos.
2) It is not adequate to define our system solely in terms of the senarius or even of the senarius limited by an index. Rather it is necessary to introduce a higher norm containing the first two norms though not identical with them. That norm consists of a harmonic model. For Pythagoras it was the fifth. For us it is the triad. *Hence in our system all relationships are defined in terms of the triad and its constituents, fifth and third.*

The road is now clear for a systematic study of the intervals. We limit ourselves to the diatonic intervals, which we define as the products and quotients of the senarius. As determined by the group S T D, we limit the 3-series by 3^2, and the 5-series by 5^1. The overall index is 45 (5×3^2). This represents the tones F-sharp and G-flat, situated at the confines of diatonic and chromatic tonalities. Triads build on diatonic values will be rated diatonic though they may include tones which, when directly related to 1, would be rated chromatic. In the key of C major, for instance, the chord of B major includes D-sharp ($3 \times 5^2 = 75$ in Just intonation), forming an augmented second with C. Understood as a "perspective" of B (15), however, it is accepted within the diatonic tonality. Relationships like this one keep the limits floating. Theoretically the line has to be drawn somewhere. The inclusion of F-sharp and G-flat among diatonic intervals is justified not only by their generation as the determinants of the second dominants but also melodically from their appearance in the "supra-major" (ascending lydian) and "infra-minor" (descending locrian) scales transposed to C:

C D E F-sharp G A B C
C B-flat A-flat G-flat F E-flat D-flat C

The diatonic intervals from C are, then, the following:

FIFTHS	THIRDS
$3^1 = G, F$	$5^1 = E,$ A-flat
$3^2 = D,$ B-flat	

FIFTHS AND THIRDS

$3^1 \cdot 5^1 = B,$ D-flat $\qquad 3^1 : 5^1 = E$-flat, A
$3^2 \times 5^1 = F$-sharp, G-flat $\qquad (3^2 : 5^1 = D,$ B-flat)

We shall now discuss the diatonic intervals and their ratios.

Fifths (3/1, 1/3). These are the dominants and have received ample attention earlier (cf. pp. 22 ff.).

Wholetones ($3^2/1, 1/3^2$). This interval, which appears between the tonic and the second dominants (C to D upward, C to B-flat downward), actually results from the relation between dominant and subdominant. The wholetone is the complement of a dominant in the opposite dominant. We call this kind of complement a *countercomplement* (symbol ¢¢).

Tonal Functions of Intervals 71

Generally we call intervals springing from the relation between reciprocal intervals *symmetric intervals* (the symbol for symmetric dominants will be ⊄D). The term *symmetric* is ambivalent, whereas the term *countercomplement* implies a predominance assigned to the fifth in which the complementation takes place. The following examples serve as illustration. If the fixed tone is *g* and the complemented tone is *f* (both in relation to *c*), we designate the interval as countercomplement of the subdominant (in the dominant) and give it the symbol ¢¢S. If the fixed tone is f_1 and the complemented tone is g_1 (both in relation to *c*), we designate the interval as countercomplement of the dominant (in the subdominant) and give it the symbol ¢¢D. When the wholetone interval shows no perceptible preponderance of one of the tones over the other, we use the term *countercomplement of symmetric dominants* and give it the symbol ¢¢ ⊄D .

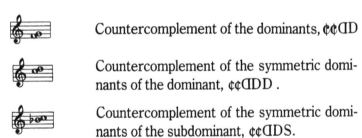

Countercomplement of the dominants, ¢¢⊄D

Countercomplement of the symmetric dominants of the dominant, ¢¢⊄DD .

Countercomplement of the symmetric dominants of the subdominant, ¢¢⊄DS.

Inversions may be indicated by the letter *I* preceding the symbol:

Note, however, that for the natural seventh the position shown above is the original one, and that the major second is the inversion.

Major thirds (5/1, 1/5). We have already introduced the determinant. Its role within the larger concept of tonality will be elucidated in the next chapter. The symmetric determinant (augmented fifth) will be treated in the last chapter in connection with its chordal form (cf. pp. 88f.).

Major sevenths (3×5, $1/3 \times 1/5$). According to its mathematical signature, the major seventh results from adding a third to a fifth. It could thus be defined as the determinant of the dominant, or the subdeterminant of the subdominant. In this way, however, the direct relation between the two tones of the interval is abandoned for an indirect one, which does not express the tension between the two tones. The concept of countercomplement sheds more light on the psychology of the interval. It points to the relation between the interval and the dominant on the opposite side: Δ: S instead of Δ + D (1/5 : 3/1 instead of 1/5 × 1/3). The countercomplement of the dominant has brought forth the wholetone. The countercomplement of the determinant brings forth the halftone. The dissonant character of the interval is a foregone conclusion to the harmonicist trained in such concepts as "opposition of the determinant" (the element determining the mode or sex of the triad) and "reciprocal dominant." Following are examples of the interval:

¢¢Δ   ¢¢∇   ¢¢Δd   ¢¢∇s

Minor thirds (3/5, 5/3). The complement of the determinant has been introduced earlier (cf. p. 23). Here are some examples illustrating the technique of using the concept and the symbols:

¢Δ   °¢∇   °¢∇d or ¢∇   °¢Δ or ¢Δs

Tritone (1/45, 45/1). Harmonically, the tritone is related to the countercomplement of the determinant inasmuch as it is also a relationship between a determinant and a counterdominant, the latter once removed (symbolized by ¢¢²).

¢¢²Δ   ¢¢²Δd²   ¢¢²∇s   ¢¢²Δd   ¢¢²∇s²

This is a very farfetched relationship indeed! We are at the confines of diatonic tonality, and one may wonder whether the *diabolus in musica* as a nickname for that dangerous interval may not have had, in the minds of those who "knew," a meaning more serious than that of mere vocal difficulty.

Tonal Functions of Intervals

Following is a synoptic table of the diatonic intervals referring to C as tonic:

8.
TONAL FUNCTIONS OF TRIADS

The world is One; it began to develop from the middle.
　　　　　　　　　　　　　　　　　　　　Philolaos

An interval is really a primitive chord. Now when we build a chord on one of the tones of an interval, the interior relationship is dimmed in favor of the outer hierarchical position. This amounts to what could be considered a sort of microscopic internal modulation:

In a system generated by the triad, denying a primary function to the third is absurd. It is high time to admit at last that determinant relations are direct functions. Recognizing solely the fifth as a primary function means applying the Pythagorean dominant norm to a triadic system. We are also inconsistent when admitting a direct relationship of the minor triad (really a derived interval) in the expression "relative chord" while denying it to the determinant.

Take an A-flat major chord in the key of C major. According to the logic of our system and the musical practice of at least the last four hundred years, it is simply the subdeterminant ∇. I am not saying that it must in all cases be so interpreted. It might be understood as the subdominant relative sR. All depends on the context. Nor do I wish the term *relative* to be banned from the harmonic vocabulary. We may continue speaking of the A-minor chord in C major as the tonic relative Tr as long as we bear in mind that the real harmonic relationship is that of the minor chord in absolute conception of the determinant $\overset{\circ}{=}\Delta$. Again, in other cases it might be understood as the minor determinant chord of the subdominant $-\Delta S$. Harmonic analysis, being an intellectualization of intuitive processes, cannot be applied in a mechanical way.

78 A Theory of Harmony

Following is a table of the functions of the triads build on the tones of diatonic tonality. The symbols written above the staff refer to major triads. The first row of symbols below the staff identifies minor triads in absolute conception ◯; the second row, in telluric adaptation ⊕:

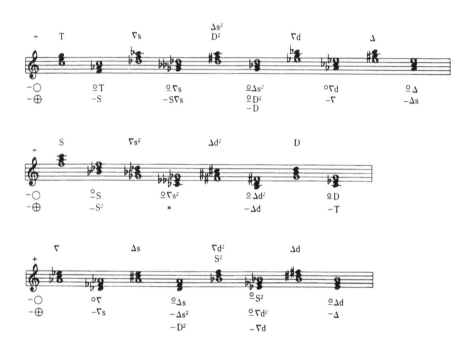

The chord marked with an asterisk (*) cannot be signed diatonically in telluric adaptation, for while G-flat is still partaking in the diatonic system, C-flat is not.

This brings up the question of chromaticism. I have hinted before at the existence of a chromatic tonality, the study of which lies outside the scope of this paper. Chromatic chord relations, however, used within an enlarged diatonic tonality should be listed here. Such chord may be signed either chromatically or diatonically. In the table below, only their diatonic signatures are indicated. The distinguishing sign of chords belonging to chromaticism is the Δ^2, which plays the role of a connecting link with diatony. In telluric adaptation, the chord of F-sharp minor belongs to diatonic tonality. Therefore in that case Δ^2 does not appear. The chords marked * are decidedly outside the possibility of being represented by the tempered system of twelve tones. They are included below in order to show the chord pair in each case. The chromatic tones on which chords are built which might be considered within an enlarged diatonic tonality are C-sharp, D-sharp, G-sharp, A-sharp, C-flat, and F-flat.

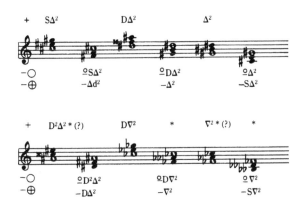

9.

TONAL FUNCTIONS OF NONTRIADIC AND COMPOUND CHORDS

And that which is made up of these two parts, the ever-moving Divine and the everchanging Mortal, that is the World.

Philolaos

Chords may be conveniently classified as follows:

    I. Indeterminate chords
    II. Determinate chords
        A. One generator
        B. Several generators
            1. Generators not coordinated
            2. Generators coordinated (polytonality)

II A comprises the triad and the natural-seventh chord. Class I and Class II B remain to be discussed.

Class I: Indeterminate Chords

The concept *chord* has been defined as a tone conglomerate organized by one or several generators. The ancient rule saying that at least three tones are required to form a chord is still valid, not unlike the proposition that three points are required to form a geometric figure. Without a third tone added to the interval of the fifth, the organizing current remains ill defined. Therefore we may characterize the fifth as a preharmonic conglomerate, a potential chord. And since adding the determinant is the preeminent way of making the fifth an element of a chord, we may call the tone conglomerates formed by the fifth and its inversion, the fourth, *indeterminate* harmonies.

Let three tones be given, spaced in fifths, e.g., f_1—c—g. Is this a directed conglomerate? It is not. The two upper tones may be interpreted as overtones of f_1; inversely, the two lower tones may be comprehended as undertones of g; again, g and f_1 may be thought of as dominants of c; finally, g and f_1 may be considered the generators of c.

Let now the three tones be spaced in fourths: g_1—c—f. In theory, nothing is changed, but in fact a directional tendency towards f will be felt. Several factors may be called upon for an explanation. We might say that in a fourth, e.g., g_1—c, the telluric adaptation in favor of g_1 is thwarted by the weight of c as the fundamental of the fifth c—g, reinforced by the position of c as top note. There might also exist a melodic influence stemming from the primary cadence dominant-tonic which tends to cancel the telluric adaptation in favor of g_1. Similar observations are valid for the three-tone conglomerate g_1—c—f, where the top note might be felt to be accompanied by the two other ones. However, while the trend thus described is undeniable, the situation remains precarious, and any one of the interpretations of three tones spaced in fifths may be brought into play. Hence we still maintain that a conglomerate of three tones spaced in fourths is preharmonic.

By increasing the number of tones while maintaining the building principle of spacing in fourths, we experience no marked change. The relative prevalence of the top note persists, while the possibilities of other interpretations increase. In this conglomerate, for instance, a tendency might be felt to understand the whole as being organized by the tones e and c^2:

We might also listen to the chord as an emanation of the tones b_1, a, and g^1. Other interpretations can be created at will.

A somewhat different situation arises from a combination of fifths and fourths:

The first chord, shown in a progression where it is used like a triad (in the sense suggested toward the end of the preceding chapter), presents itself as formed by two generators, b_2-flat and c^1. Nevertheless, a concep-

Tonal Function of Nontriadic and Compound Chords

tion of fifths ascending from b_2-flat (b_2-flat, f_1, c, g, d^1) or ascending and descending from c (b_2-flat, f_1, c, g, d^1) is in no way to be excluded. We note that while the determinant of the bass note is present, its role as determinant is doubtful. Such uncertainties may be responsible for the peculiar iridescence of this and similar chords, which accounts for their peculiar fascination.

Three successive fifths may be arranged not only in fifths and fourths but also within the space of one fifth. In this arrangement, a tone may occupy three different positions. The three corresponding reciprocations are remarkable for being composed of the same notes as the original positions, because the conglomerate itself is built of reciprocated tones (dominants):

In this form of assembling three fifths, there appears a slight prevalence, namely, that of the spatially isolated tone. If this interpretation is accepted, then the tones forming the interval of the second become the symmetric dominants (D of the isolated tone, which in turn is understood as generator. Hence we may assign functions according to the generators:

D T T T S(?) T D T

Functional interpretation, however, remains particularly precarious in indeterminate harmony.

Class II B, 1: Determinate Chords
with Several Not Coordinated Generators

This section includes the potentially largest variety of chords. To approach anything like a comprehensive study, even in a work not confined to a mere exposition of principles like this paper, is impossible. Discussion of a few cases of special interest must suffice.

86   *A Theory of Harmony*

Compound chords may be built from the following building units and their combinations:

  (a) Triads and natural-seventh chords
  (b) Thirds
  (c) Seconds

(a) Triads and natural-seventh chords

(i) The generation of this chord is shown here:

It is a bisexual chord, produced by the major tonic C and (in absolute conception) the minor determinant. Minor is prevalent in the first of the following two positions; major, in the second:

(ii) In terms of C major, this chord is a truncated form of the full determinant:

The incompleteness on the major side accentuates the prevalence of the minor side, to which telluric adaptation has already conferred preponderance. This chord may be thought of as the explicit form of the counter-complement of the minor determinant, ¢¢−Δ.

(iii) The reciprocal form of (ii) in the sense that here the minor side is truncated. Transposed to the same pitch as (ii), the chord reads:

Tonal Function of Nontriadic and Compound Chords 87

The signature is essentially the same as in (ii) except that the preponderance of major should be expressed as $+\Delta$. As presented here transposed to C major, the signature is $+\overset{\circ}{\Delta}{}^2 S$.

(iv) Top and bottom notes are generators, producing an interpenetrating major-minor chord pair:

With C as tonic, the signature is $\overset{\circ}{{}_{+\Delta S}}\Delta^2$. With A as tonic, the signature is simply $\overset{\circ}{{}_{+T}}\Delta D$.

The next three examples concern so-called ninth chords:

       v   vi   vii

(v) The major-ninth chord consists of two interpenetrating natural-seventh chords:

The tonic may be determined by the tendencies of the components. In F major, we identify the chord as $\overset{\circ}{\Delta S_7}$. In D major, we identify the chord $\dfrac{-S_7}{SS^7}$ or $\dfrac{\overset{\circ}{T_7}}{SS^7}$.

(vi) The genesis of this chord is readily understood by looking at the table on page 48 (where other compound chords may also be found). The chord in question extends between 8/6 to 8/8 and 6/8 to 8/8, being part of a compound stretching from 8/4 to 8/8 and 4/8 to 8/8. Remembering that C major and F minor, stemming from the same generator, tend toward each other, we resolve the chord so that each element follows its proper tendency:

In the following cadence, we first hear the chord as given. Then comes the full version of the reciprocal seventh chords; the tones *F* in the upper chord and *G* in the lower chord (the respective fifths) are eliminated to

88   *A Theory of Harmony*

avoid the friction of a major second—tones, moreover, heard in the preceding chord. The final chord offers the full resolution (without E to avoid the friction of a minor second)—an ontic chord *par excellence* realizing C in both directions:

(vii) This diminished-seventh chord and the minor-ninth chord are the same; the difference resides in the degree of truncation. The tendencies of the components converge on the tonic F.

(b) Thirds

By letting a tone generate a mutually reciprocal determinant-pair, we obtain the symmetric determinant chord ⋈. There are two possible primary interpretations: diatonic and chromatic. The former confers the quality of generator to the central tone:

The latter confers that quality to the outer tones:

We are concerned only with the diatonic view, but it appears at once that the iridescent effect of the chord is in part due to its floating between the diatonic and chromatic worlds. (Incidentally, sounding the chord on the sonometer—1/1, 4/5, 16/25—will be a surprise to anybody never having heard it in Just intonation. There is a marvellous and mysterious quality to its sound, which gives me the distinct feeling of penetrating into another dimension of tone. Typical examples occur in Liszt's *Faust* Symphony and Strauss's *Also sprach Zarathustra*.) The operations of complementation and counter-complementation may be applied to the symmetric determinant chord but cannot be discussed here. It should be

Tonal Function of Nontriadic and Compound Chords

mentioned, however, that the wholetone scale may be considered the melodic projection of two symmetric determinant chords ⋈:

We disregard the chromatic tonality into which the structure penetrates. The wholetone scale is an "adominantic" scale, just as the pentatonic scale is indeterminate. The dominantic system is indeterminate, whereas the wholetone scale is transdominantic. The dominantic system is presexual, whereas the transdominantic system is due to the exclusive action of the "sexualizing" interval.

(c) Seconds

Seconds may appear as the spatial result of various harmonic operations, such as countercomplementing the dominants, inverting the natural seventh, or combining symmetric determinant chords. Of special importance are chords the characteristic part of which is encompassed by a tritone. Here are two examples (in the key of C):

Another reciprocal pair of tritonic chords looks like the truncated natural-seventh chord in different inversions, but the meaning is not the same:

These chords realize the countercomplement of the two dominants and moreover contain their respective determinants. The combination of the two chords reveals the harmonic origin of *D*-flat (in C major), generally interpreted as an "altered" fifth of the dominant:

One wonders whether the chord of the natural seventh does not draw additional force from the simultaneous presence of both dominants.

Here are some other progressions involving the tritone:

These chords are best explained in terms of the preponderance of one element of the countercomplement rather than in terms of a deceptive cadence. In the first case, the note *a* prevails; in the second case, the note *b*. In a combination of the two chords, the quality of the major second characteristic of the countercomplement is dimmed by the force of the determinants:

The two determinants may be interpreted as truncated natural-seventh chords, which explains their primary tendencies toward A minor and E major:

Closely related to the preceding examples is the famous "Tristan chord":

Undoubtedly *g*-sharp is an apoggiatura. Nevertheless, a literal analysis of the first chord cannot be dispensed with; for during the long sounding of the chord, a direct harmonic appreciation is experienced which, together with the melodic appreciation, accounts to a high degree for the ambiguous character of the chord, one of its beauties. From mere listening, the chord could be interpreted as:

In absolute conception, this is the minor subdominant of D-sharp major or perhaps also the complement of the tonic, both with an added seventh.

This is certainly one part of the compound. Another explanation relates the chord to the key of A, in which it functions as the minor subdominant (represented by f and b_1 with the later addition of a). Hence the primary tendencies of the complete compound are:

I am inclined to see a connection between this implicit D-sharp = E-flat chord and the A-flat love duet in the second act. The key of A-flat would then be the tonic of the "invisible" dominant (E-flat), with D-sharp and G-sharp enharmonically changed to, respectively, E-flat and A-flat. In this connection, note the enharmonic change of A-flat to G-sharp later in the duet!

Class II B, 2: Determinate Chords with Several Coordinated Generator

This section deals exclusively with polytonality. A brief enunciation of principles must suffice. Strictly speaking, polytonality means coexistence of several systems (at least two), neither of which is subordinate to the other. Now in the presence of two coordinated keys we cannot conceive of a common frame of reference; for if the two coordinated keys were referred to a third one, we would not speak of polytonality but rather of functional simultaneity. All we can do in the case of polytonality is find out the reciprocal relationship expressed in terms of keys, spatial distance, or harmonic proportions—in short, all we can do is state a certain kind of nonidentity. In practice, polytonality in such a literal sense may be used only for short stretches, not only because it is a tiresome device, but mainly because through telluric influence it is an effect most difficult to maintain for any length of time. The following example is a case in point:

Theoretically speaking, the two keys, C major and D-flat major, are coordinated. Their reciprocal harmonic relation can be simply stated:

$$\text{D-flat to C} = \nabla S$$
$$\text{C to D-flat} = \Delta D$$

The impression, however, is one of preponderance of the tone and chord C over the melody. Hence definition in terms of C major is adequate: $\nabla S \atop T$.

Summary

1. Tone has a structure. Its validity can be tested on the physical-acoustical level (division of the string) as well as on the musical-esthetic level (fertility and musical adequacy of application).

2. Major and minor are manifestations of the general principle of polarity.

3. The triad being the norm of our tonal system, the third has a direct function within the tonality, equal in dignity to the fifth. Parallel to the term *dominants* for the upper and lower fifths, the term *determinants* will serve for the functions of the third.

4. A major triad tends to function as dominant, a minor triad as subdominant.

5. A chord is a conglomerate organized by one or several generators.

6. To distinguish natural from psychological consonance and dissonance, the concept pair *ontic-gignetic* will designate the latter.

7. The seventh in the dominant seventh chord is the natural seventh.

8. In analogy to calling the fourth the *complement* of the fifth in the octave, the minor third is recognized as the complement of the determinant in the fifth.

9. Temperament arises from the necessity to represent the infinite within the definite.

10. Traditional and newly introduced nomenclature is indicated by shorthand symbols.

APPENDIX A
Examples to Chapter 8

Examples illustrating the use of our nomenclature:

Examples of function interpretation:

Here (3) is related to (2). But a different situation exists in the following version where (3) appears related to the dominant:

At * in the next example, it would seem preferable to say $\circ$ T instead of −S, the chord being so to speak a nuance of the preceding one. The impression is due mainly to the pedal effect which prevents us from understanding the chord change as a true succession.

In the progression below, (3) proceeds from (2), hence $\circ$ ∇ rather than −∇s. The interpretation of the next chords hinges on the enharmonic change *f*-flat to *e*, hence (4) is understood as dependent on *E*: $\circ$ ∆

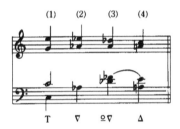

Functional symbols of tones may also be applied in progressions of nontriadic chords. Such chords are then used in lieu of triads. Once the nature of the chords is established (see chapter 9), they may be regarded as units, and their functions are then determined solely by the tones on which they are built:

When a progression of identical chords, triadic or nontriadic, is determined mainly by melody, as in this example:

it seems to me that only points where melodic and harmonic impulses join should be signed. This may be done as shown in the example or even by leaving out the middle signature and marking only the principal pillars, i.e., only the first and last chords.

APPENDIX B

Comments on the Text by Hugo Kauder

Page	Comment
4	In tone, quantity and quality coincide into one: pitch defined physically as a vibration quantum is yet a quality. Thus tone—and equally musical number—is a symbol, that is, an identity of the ideal and the real.
6	Overtones: a spiritual principle reveals itself as an event of nature. The agreement of the two we call *natural law*. Observing it is *science*, applying it is *art*.
13	Not merely longer (beginning with Pythagoras and Heraclitus) but also more authoritative (Goethe!).
14	The number 5 signifies a limit in the presentation of three-dimensional space: only five regular bodies are possible, and their numbers coincide with the musical numbers.
14	Measure and value.
15	Polarity: not above–below but centrifugal–centripetal. What in earthly (=human) perspective appears as opposition of above and below, appears in cosmic perspective as opposition centripetal-centrifugal. Cf. p. 27.
15	. . . as triad *under C,* that is, with descending major third.
15	It is not based on polarity, it is (seemingly) opposed to polarity.
16	The downward division of the upper octave to gain the fourth c^1-*f-c appears* forced but in reality results from the principle of polarity. The subdominant is in fact the opposite pole of the dominant. Like every individual (already the atom!), also the scale is *bipolar.*
16	This "alteration" of the third affects generally the subdominant, which reveals its true nature indeed only as a minor chord (the *Gegenklang* of the tonic).
17	The "absolute conception" is the cadence [formed] by the un-

dertones on *E* (tonic)-*B* (upper dominant)-*A* (lower dominant):

17	It is not a compromise between the two theories but must be recognized as *basic fact* that music is subject not only to the law of polarity but equally so to the law of gravity and of organic life. The direction of these two is *irreversible*.
21	Attention!! This "agglomeration" is caused by a melodic motion. For a sufficient definition of the concept *chord*, everything must be promptly eliminated that is not a chord.
22	Theoretically the generator contains also the undertones. Their not being physically realizable is irrelevant for the theory.
22	Bruckner's Ninth, end of the first movement; *Te Deum*, beginning and end.
23	To avoid confusion: *third, fifth,* etc. are ordinal numbers, a mere counting of a quasi-spatial tone sequence (scale). The tone numbers indicate relations.
25	Cadence as a "dialectic process" (M. Hauptmann): T=thesis, S=antithesis, D-T=synthesis. That is: the subdominant puts into question the tonic, the dominant restores it. In this respect one can consider the complete cadence as a definitive conclusion.
25	In absolute conception, upper and lower dominants have exchanged their meanings. The terms *dominant* and *counterdominant* would be valid for both modes. $D = \pm V$. $CD = \mp V$.
30	Does the cadence receive its full meaning only by being coordinated with the scale? Otherwise one remains with a traversal of the circle of fifths with fluctuating tonality. A "pure" theory of chords should, however, exclude as far as possible the concept of scale.
46f.	According to polarity, it would be more consistent to show the seventh in both chords as "passing."

47	According to Riemann, these are sixth chords $-d_6$ and $+f^6$ (chord of the *sixte ajoutée,* Rameau).
53	Also with tones played staccato we experience the *space* between them. The concept of the continuum is primary, not the continuum itself.
53	Frequency=measure. Musical pitch=value.
53	The Greeks did not do it when naming the notes (successive letters of the alphabet!), yet when naming the scale steps (e.g., hypatē hypaton and hypatē meson, etc.).
54	Octave as totality of tonal relationships, diapasōn.
60	More: it is the viewpoint of nihilism!

www.ingramcontent.com/pod-product-compliance
Lightning Source LLC
Chambersburg PA
CBHW032100120425
24981CB00023B/138